Theory
of
type design

Theory
of
type design

Gerard Unger

nai010

Contents

Foreword

Gerry Leonidas

We can evaluate the maturity of a field of knowledge by considering four questions: first, are the boundaries of its focus, and – consequently – its positioning and relationships with other fields, clear and well understood? Second, is there a body of knowledge that is accepted as foundational for all activity by the community active in the field? Third, are there established routes for learning and practicing in the field? And fourth, are there established paths for research, reflection, knowledge generation and correction in the field?

To different degrees, type design is a nascent field across all four aspects. It utilises craft and software skills, with methodologies that combine empirical and experimental modes. It requires an understanding of typography and communication design, while success relies heavily on an understanding of both cultural and business aspects. This activity is taking place within an uneven distribution of reference texts, which spans disciplines. A typeface designer will be expected to read about the history of printing and documents, the impact of changing technologies on communication practice, and to be aware of societal trends, while constantly updating themself on an evolving environment in the support of texts on devices. A smattering of theoretical texts tend to be selective in their focus, and their relevance to practice is not easily understood.

The last twenty years have seen an accelerating growth in formal education in typeface design, from short courses to full postgraduate programmes, and an expanding community of PhD researchers; but there is considerable variation between both curricula and objectives, with significant variations internationally. And, lastly, there are only hints for progression paths across the various careers connected to typeface design. Those interested in expanding knowledge in the field often have to map their own routes, and work without the support in resources that a mature discipline would provide.

Into this environment of gradual positive change comes the book you are holding in your hands: it is, with no exaggeration, the first of its kind. It addresses all four questions I raised above, and has the potential to transform both education and discourse in type design.

The book's key achievement is to encapsulate concisely the totality of the deliberations that inform the process of type design. It enables learners to structure their thinking about their practice, by developing an understanding of the conceptual elements that go into a designer's decisions. At a higher level of discourse, it can be used as a starting point for structuring discussions on genre, convention, innovation, and originality in type design. By providing a framework and a terminology for the different considerations and decisions that go into a typeface, it makes a huge leap towards disambiguating a practice that has hidden behind personal narratives and subjective interpretations for decades – for this alone it would be invaluable, and overdue.

Equally valuable is the book's achievement of being accessible while not underestimating its reader. It distils decades of research and experience into an eminently readable text that informs and challenges, but does not intimidate or confuse the reader. A wide range of references and thought processes are explained in the context of practice in a manner that is relevant to learners, practitioners, educators, and researchers alike. The rich illustrations make the connections to practice evident, and exemplify scholarship that respects its audience.

This last point is critical in the evaluation of the *Theory of Type Design*: it places itself at the centre of a field where wider narratives are scarce, and works that synthesize historical research, the discussion of practice, and reflection on decision-making are practically non-existent. As such, it offers a reference point for the design community to respond to, and, not least, for other authors to contribute further. It provides a model for writing that recognizes personal experience, but does not place it at the centre of the narrative, instead weaving it into a wider examination of the discipline. And, as such, it offers a text for members of other disciplines to engage with.

For all of these reasons, this book is a significant step in the progress of type design towards being an established knowledge discipline. In our field, I can think of no greater compliment.

Acknowledgements

My interest in the theoretical aspects of typography and type design – and thus the beginning of this theory – was first nurtured by my father's bookcase and in the bookshop of Hijman, Stenfert Kroese & Van der Zande in Arnhem, my hometown. It has been stimulated by some of my teachers at the Gerrit Rietveld Academy, especially Theo Kurpershoek, and by Professor G.W. Ovink of the University of Amsterdam, who was also advisor to the Amsterdam Typefoundry and librarian of its Typographic Library. Also I owe much to the generosity and clear opinions of my first boss, Wim Crouwel, and over many years to the patience of students, who were prepared to listen to my observations and almost always gave something stimulating in return.

My involvement by Michael Twyman in the Department of Typography & Graphic Communication at the University of Reading has been very important for me. Over many years the observations and criticism of Marjan, my wife, have helped to shape and sharpen my thoughts. I have to thank many more people for exchanges of ideas, stimulating conversations, and glimpses into different worlds of design. I thank Gerry Leonidas who, by keeping me active in the MA Typeface Design at Reading and by reading and reshuffling early drafts of this theory, contributed to the final result. Thanks also to Christopher Burke for inspiring conversations and for his careful editing of this theory.

I am very grateful to all who have contributed fonts and illustrations: Nadine Chahine and Bill Davis of Monotype, Elena Schneider, Zuzana Licko and Rudy VanderLans of Emigre, Dan Rhatigan of Adobe, Jürgen Siebert of FontShop, Thibault Baralon, Elena Papassissa, Alisa Nowak, Veronika Burian and José Scaglione Of TypeTogether, Florian Runge and Rosetta, Matthew Carter and Cherie Cone (Carter & Cone), Michael Twyman, Vaibhav Singh, Gerry Leonidas, Mohamad Dakak, Gerrit Noordzij, Jeremy Tankard, Jean-François Porchez, Kai Bernau and Commercial, Remco van Bladel, Nicole Dotin and the Process Type Foundry, Fred Smeijers, Anna-Lisa Schönecker, Pierre di Sciullo, Peter Matthias Noordzij and TEFF, Maarten Evenhuis, Bas Jacobs and Underware, Lee Yuen-Rapati, Rickey Tax and Museum Meermanno, Mathieu Lommen and the Special Collections at the University of Amsterdam Library, Guy Hutsebaut of the Museum Plantin-Moretus, Erik van Blokland and Just van Rossum, Jonathan Hoefler of Hoefler & Co., Sebastian Losch, Neville Brody and Brody Associates, Riccardo Olocco, Hansje van Halem, Gijs Bakker, Irma Boom.

1   Prologue

Of all designed objects, letters are probably the most pervasive, very familiar yet amazingly diverse in their appearance. Letterforms range from the almost anonymous and utilitarian in large quantities to a few individual and exceptional shapes. Between such extremes, designers have devised almost all possible variations; there seems to be no limit to human ingenuity when it comes to varying letterforms.

While decorated initials and ornaments were always part of the repertoire of printing types (following the example of manuscripts), nineteenth-century readers witnessed a spectacular increase in typographic diversity. This was the consequence of several developments, including the industrialization of printing, the growth of cities and readership, and the advent of advertising. Such events brought with them, among many whimsical designs, sanserif typefaces and Egyptians.[a] In the 1960s and 1970s phototypesetting, with digital typesetting on its heels,[b] liberated type from the restrictions of metal – another incentive for variation. And in the late 1980s easy-to-use type design programs led again to an increase in diversity. The resulting typographic profusion seems to be taken for granted nowadays – which deserves a study in itself.

a] Egyptians are typefaces with slab-serifs and often with little difference between thick and thin parts. They first appeared between 1815 and 1820. See Gray (1976), pp 25, 26. The development of imaginative and even fantastic, multi-coloured letterforms was stimulated in particular by the invention and rapid spread of lithography (invented in 1796).

b] The first digital typesetting machine, the Digiset of Dr.-Ing. Rudolf Hell GmbH, was introduced to the printing industry in 1965.

A theory of type design therefore has to take a broad view, however difficult it may seem to embrace in a single approach all aspects of the design of letterforms (plus accompanying signs) and of their interpretations, from everyday typographic workhorses to rare and entirely personal shapes. Although many type designers are very practical, a theory of type design is definitely of use, as it will broaden insights and can benefit the quality of the profession by stimulating debate. To achieve this, theory should not be merely descriptive; it should certainly not be prescriptive, but investigative and reflective. Such a theory should also be critical, an enquiry into the concepts, notions and ideas we use in making sense of letterforms.[1]

Type designers love to handle letterforms and leave their stamps on them, and they like to explore the possibilities of their tools, now often entirely digital. There is also a wide interest in the history of type-making, both technologically and stylistically, and in other subjects related to letterforms, such as legibility research. This theory explores and explains as much of type design as possible, in the course of which it will be seen that some basic questions still lack clear or complete answers – for example, about the processing of letterforms in the brain.

Although this theory will hit upon a few uncertainties, most subjects related to type design have been well researched and recorded. This theory will not go deeply into specialized areas, such as the history of punchcutting, but it will reflect on the importance of the history of type design and historical models for design practice. Other subjects will be treated similarly. This theory is not a DIY-course[2] but it will broadly outline the design process and explain why new type designs continue to be made. And this theory mainly concerns the Latin script.

Type design has been a field of systematic study for a long time.[3] In 1886, for example, *Historic Printing Types* by the American printer Theodore Low De Vinne (1828–1914) was published, and in 1900 his *Plain Printing Types* appeared, including a treatise on type-making. These days professional practice and research go together on an equal footing, informing and complementing each other.[c] This is only natural, considering all the changes that type design has undergone since the end of the nineteenth century.

c] In 2013 Gerry Leonidas asked me during my PhD ceremony: 'How do you suggest that your thesis provides a model for practice-based research in typeface design that can contribute to this process ... of professional activity and research coexisting and complementing each other?' This theory, finally, is my answer.

Type design is, obviously, the design of typefaces, which are often called fonts. But a font is (or was) a complete set of characters in one single style or weight: for instance, all the characters in the bold italic version of a particular typeface. And a typeface is a collection of fonts with the same identity, with stylistic correspondences, which is also called a type family.[d] Type was the term used for metal letters, to refer to them collectively or generally, as in typecasting or a typewriter. It is now also used for digitally made letters and other typographic signs. Terminology features prominently in this theory, as it is an important tool for clarity. The terminology of type design and typography is sometimes vague: for example, the word 'roman', which – with an initial capital – refers to ancient Roman letterforms. Without an inital capital, roman can denote a classical typeface with serifs, and a modern one as well, such as *Times New Roman* (1932); or it signifies upright as opposed to italic, and is sometimes even used as synonymous with regular.

d] In the days of metal type a font (or fount) was a set of characters of one specific style or weight in one size, for example 10 point, to fill a typecase. Since the introduction of scalable fonts, with Postscript in 1984, a font allows for many different type sizes. Typefaces in metal often consisted of three or four fonts: roman, italic, bold, and bold italic. By the end of the nineteenth century this had become more or less the standard, which was then fixed by the manufacturers of typesetting machines. In the twentieth century experiments began with treating different typefaces as one design, for example faces with and without serifs. An early example is the Romulus family (1931–1937) by the Dutch designer Jan van Krimpen; see Dreyfus (1952), pp 36–46. From the mid 1980s, with the advent of digital type design, the type family began to grow in number of variations and weights, with OpenType Variable Fonts (2016) offering many more possibilities.

These are, admittedly, minor hurdles in putting together a theory of type design. In 2006 the second edition of my book *Terwijl je leest* was published, dealing with what happens when we read – the interaction of type, eyes, brain, and mind.[4] Several years ago, one of the students at the University of Reading on the MA Typeface Design told me that she had left her mother in Germany puzzled about what exactly she was studying. After she gave her mother the German version of my book, *Wie man's liest* (2009), to read, the reaction was: 'Now I understand'. While this is very gratifying, I intend to go much further with this theory. I expect that students will read it, few mothers, and some colleagues – not all of them are eager theorists.[e] I have often been asked what my profession is (not only by my once future father-in-law), and I always need to explain: the obvious answer is 'I'm a type designer', which is mostly met with a blank stare. When I add 'fonts' – aah – then it is clear. This is how far the general public may go.

With some fifty years of experience in observing and handling letterforms, both practically and theoretically, designing and teaching, I think that I am in a position to put together an orderly, clear and comprehensive theory of type design – while it is inevitable that this theory will have to be adapted and expanded due to further technological developments, for example.

e] According to Peter Bilak it is unlikely that a theory of type design will ever be compiled. 'Type design, however, seems to resist attempts to establish an encompassing theory by its very nature. Type design is not an intellectual activity, but relies on a gesture of the person and his ability to express it formally. Even if a theory existed, it would not be very useful, since type design is governed by practice.' – http://www.peterbilak.com/site/texts.php?id=100 (21/06/2017).

1. Culler (2000), pp 14, 15.
2. Henestrosa *et al.* (2017), *passim*. This publication is a good DIY-course.
3. Morison (1963), pp ix–xxix. Since Morison wrote this introduction much has been added to what he called 'critical bibliography'.
4. Unger (2007), *passim*.

workhorse
plodder

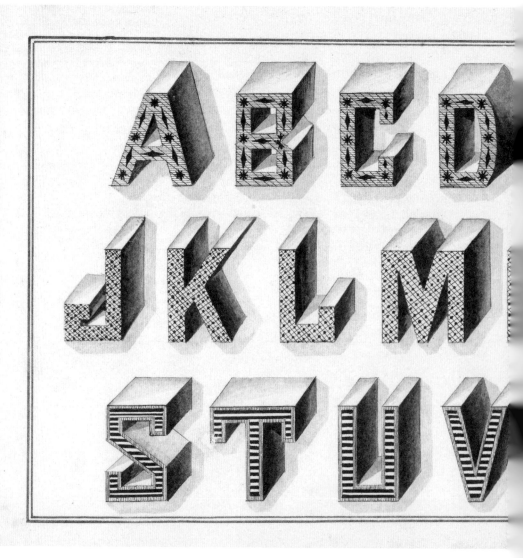

Spoken Georgian is like no other language you are likely to hear. It belongs to its own ancient linguistic group unlike any other language spoken outside the region. It includes rare sounds that many visitors may never have heard before. Some consonants, for example, are pronounced from the back of the throat with a sudden guttural puff of air.

◀ A utilitarian and multifunctional typeface: Matthew Carter, Georgia, 1996, Microsoft.

▼ An example of the spectacular increase in typographic diversity in the nineteenth century, c. 1855, 15.5 × 31.5 cm.
From: Joh. Missillie, *Verzameling van letter en ten gebruike voor schilders en teekenaars*, c. 1855, manuscript.
Information in: Mathieu Lommen, *Nederlandse belettering: negentiende eeuwse modelboeken*, 2015, De Buitenkant. SPECIAL COLLECTIONS, UNIVERSITY OF AMSTERDAM LIBRARY

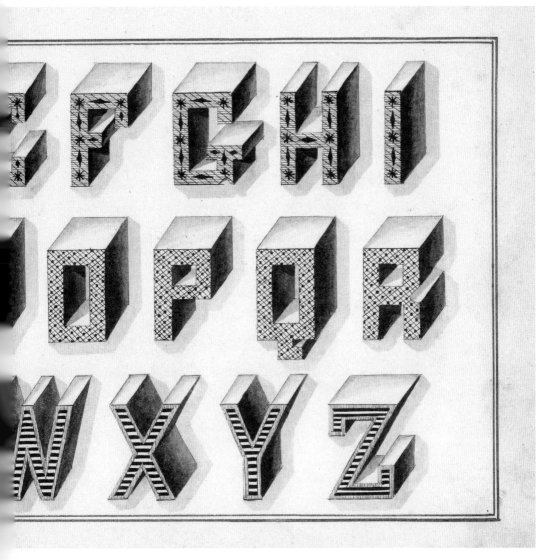

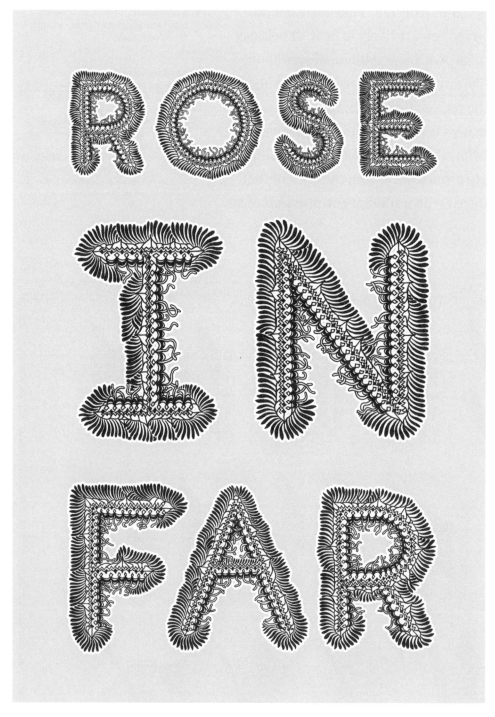

▲ Some idiosyncratic letterforms,
 Hansje van Halem i.c.w. Mathias Reynoird, 2010

THE PRACTICE OF

TYPOGRAPHY

A TREATISE ON THE
PROCESSES OF TYPE-MAKING
THE POINT SYSTEM, THE NAMES, SIZES
STYLES AND PRICES OF

PLAIN PRINTING TYPES

BY

THEODORE LOW DE VINNE

NEW YORK
THE CENTURY CO.
1900

▲ Theodore Low De Vinne, *Plain Printing Types*, a volume of: *The Practice of Typography*, 1900, The Century Co., 19 × 12.8 cm.

▲ A complete set of characters in one single style and weight. Gerard Unger, *Alverata* regular, 2013, TypeTogether.

2 The nature of type design

In an endeavour to make clear what design essentially is, it has been separated from craft (and art).[1] A clear and simple description of design is: 'The planning and drawing of something before it is made'.[a] Design is primarily functional and usually geared to mass-production – you need to collaborate with others to realize the design[2] – a way of working in the automobile industry, for example, and also in the graphic industry after the mechanization of casting and composing type at the end of the nineteenth century. From then on designing typefaces meant only planning and sketching or drawing them, as they were produced by people other than the designer.[b] Products of craft are essentially hand-made: whether it is a table, a vase, or lettering cut in stone, everything is done by one person from planning to realization.[3]

Since the advent of digital design in the mid-1980s the planning, sketching, and drawing of typefaces can be done on screen with a hand-held instrument, and digitization has brought production – the finishing of fonts and preparing these for various applications – into the hands of designers. Digital typefaces can be mass-produced – many are mass-used – and some are planned for a specific function. For both design and production, cooperation with others is possible, although many typefaces are planned and executed by designers themselves, including the extension of character sets for many different languages, and the preparation of fonts for use in print and on the web.

Still, creating letterforms on screen is often preceded by sketching, drawing, and writing on paper with pencils and different kinds of pens, painting with brushes, sculpting, cutting in stone or wood, cutting models from paper, and more – all craft-like activities. Making typefaces is design with aspects of craft;[c] the two have blended, as is the case with the design and production of many other objects, such as chairs that can be represented three-dimensionally on screen and produced privately in small numbers with a 3D-printer.

a] The printed edition (2002) of the *Shorter Oxford English Dictionary* gives as a meaning of the verb 'design': 'make drawings and plans for the construction or production of (a building, machine, garment, etc.).'

b] Southall (2005), pp 26–34. The invention of typography entailed a division of labor, long before mechanization. Type was made by hand – punches were cut, matrices struck, and type cast from them – but these tasks were not always performed by the same person. (See Moxon, 1978, p 151.) Together with typesetting, printing, and binding the whole process was industrial in character, with a division of labor.

c] In itself, punchcutting has all the aspects of a craft.

A similar blending occurs between calligraphy, lettering, and type design. Calligraphy ranges from beautiful or embellished writing to 'a visual art related to writing'.[4] A difference between calligraphy and lettering is that often the first is executed 'in one stroke ... as opposed to built-up lettering'.[5] Lettering is creating an image of a word (or several words) by sketching, drawing or painting letters, and lettering can be shaped digitally on screen as well.[6] Calligraphers leave direct traces [see chapter 9], clearly showing the characteristics of a writing instrument, while letterers form their shapes indirectly, in several phases from sketch to final result – multi-coloured, shadowed, seemingly in 3D, or with other effects. Solutions for letterforms or their details (e.g. connections of curves to stems) created with calligraphy, can be applied in a type design, and out of a few letterforms drawn for a unique occasion a lettering artist can make a complete typeface for general use – again a mix of activities.[7]

It is often claimed that type designers need a proper training in calligraphy. An elementary knowledge of the effects of handling both the broad-nibbed and the pointed pen is certainly helpful in understanding important characteristics of letterforms, although it is not necessary to be a calligrapher before becoming a type designer.

The purpose of design in general is, of course, to create objects that enable specific actions and meet specific needs, which are, when it comes to typefaces: reading and taking in the contents of texts for information gathering, recreation, and other reasons. However, type designs do not only fulfill such tasks. Another function is to help us orientate ourselves on the basis of their diversity and associated meanings [see chapter 19]. The world would be less interesting and navigable if all the messages around us would be uniformly designed with one single typeface. In this way type designs can affect communal and individual identities. Typefaces do this subliminally in small sizes and often manifestly in large sizes – type designs carry all kinds of messages on top of their primary function, which is to be legible [see chapter 21]. Entire scripts such as Cyrillic, Arabic, or Devanagari (and the Latin script as well) do this on a larger scale and much more powerfully.

Type design can begin with a plan, such as a list of features or a description of the purpose of the design. You can start with angular or round letterforms, wide or narrow, quiet or lively, and a multitude of further possibilities. Purposes or applications can vary from signage to literary books, from helping early readers, to setting an atmosphere with headlines on a fashion website. Thinking about a concept is often combined with forming visual ideas tentatively. Sketching raises questions and leads to research – sketching is research.

Only rarely is a type design developed from scratch, with a completely fresh approach, as if the designer were a *tabula rasa* (blank sheet) without any letterforms imprinted on her or his memory. Almost always a plan grows out of searching among existing themes and designs [see chapter 7], with an eye to their details and mostly without questioning their basic or conventional shapes, which are often accepted as fixed or permanent [see chapter 6]. All type designers have experience as readers and their recollections range from carefully scrutinized letterforms to fleeting shapes seen in passing.

From an active engagement with your own personal knowledge and with documentation such as type specimens, ideas will emerge and grow, and well known structural components can be considered: for example, an old face structure [see chapter 4], monolinearity or a geometrical underpinning, a sanserif, or an Egyptian with rectangular or trapezoidal serifs. There are many more approaches – the number of characteristics to choose from and their combinations is enormous, practically without end. Type designers build on such choices and combinations of samples, and vary these and make them their own, though sometimes examples are followed closely without much of a personal contribution.

Thanks to digitization, the design process now offers great flexibility, with the possibility to experiment, modify, refine, and correct for as long and as much as a designer wishes: curves with different dynamics can be tried, horizontal and vertical proportions can be varied, ultra thin and extra black versions can be made with any number of interpolated versions in between. All such possibilities can be reviewed on screen or printed out, much enlarged, in small sizes, and in different typographic settings.

While the technology for type design and the design process have changed fundamentally, letterforms have changed very little with the transition from tangible and analog type to digital and immaterial shapes. Just as we have no problem recognizing and reading the letterforms of Nicolas Jenson (c. 1420–1480), so he would be able to read most present-day typefaces.

---

1. Forsey (2005), *passim.*
2. Forsey (2013), pp 60, 68.
3. Forsey (2005), p 59.
4. https://en.wikipedia.org/wiki/Calligraphy (20/12/2016).
5. http://encyclopedia.thefreedictionary.com/Calligraphy (20/12/2016).
6. Flor (2016), p 13 & pp 118–127.
7. Flor (2016), pp 118–127.

lazy

naehtt

ageddy

more
between
a 'flick'
and
a loaded
brush

as the Bembo.
Spade

▲ Sketches by Jeremy Tankard, *Kingfisher*, 2001, 21 × 29.6 cm.

HELLA S·HAASE EEN NIEUWER TESTA- MENT

Dit boek maakt honderdduizend maaimachines overbodig. Niet de giganten waarmee de boer tijd en mankracht moet sparen, maar wel al die brommers in onze tuinen. In onze tuin, waar wij juist veel tijd en energie voor over hebben, is de maaimachine een averechte investering. Maar wat moet je anders: maaien met de zeis was immers veel te moeilijk voor gewone mensen. En over de techniek van het maaien heette het: je kunt het of je kunt het niet.

Glass Collection المقتنيات الزجاجية Blue Gilded Flask دورق أزرق مذهب ذهب وزجاج سوريا (الرقة)، أواسط القرن Syria (Raqqa), mid-12th century الثاني عشر. صُنع هذا الدورق الأزرق المذهب في أو قرب ما يعرف اليوم بمدينة This gilded blue الرقة السورية، الواقعة على نهر الفرات شمال شرق البلاد flask was made in or near what is today the small Syrian city of Raqqa, situated on the Euphrates in the north-east of the country. في أواسط القرن الثاني عشر الميلادي كانت المدينة مركزًا زاهرًا لإنتاج الخزف والزجاج. وكان يغذي هذه الصناعة ظهور الحرفيين المبدعين الهاربين من مناطق الإمبراطورية الفاطمية المتداعية In the mid-12th century AD, the city was a thriving centre for the production of pottery and glass, constantly refreshed by the appearance of craftsmen leaving the ailing Fatimid Empire.

▲ Calligraphy: Gerrit Noordzij's handwriting. Actual size.
From: Gerrit Noordzij, *Zeis en sikkel*, 1979, Bert Bakker.

◀ Lettering on a book cover by Theo Kurpershoek, teacher at the Gerrit Rietveld Academy, who taught Gerard Unger about type. 13 × 21 cm.
Hella Haasse, *Een nieuwer testament*, 1966, Querido.

▲ Mohamad Dakak, *Jali*, 2016, matching Arabic and Latin typefaces designed for signage. MA Typeface Design of the University of Reading.

▲ Dutch road sign. Typeface: Gerard Unger,
1997, ANWB.

Vette Egyptienne.

No. 478, corps 7. Minimum 3 kilo.

Amsterdamsche Lettergieterij, Galvanoplastie, Hout- en Metaalgravure
1345 BLOEMGRACHT, AMSTERDAM. 6789

No. 479, corps 10. Minimum 4 kilo.

Zooeven verschenen: F. Meijsel, Hoe rijmt dat op elkaar?
1345 ARNHEM, DOETINCHEM. 6789

No. 480, corps 14. Minimum 5½ kilo.

Amsterd. Lettergieterij, Bloemgracht 134
5 STERKE MACHINES. 6

No. 481, corps 20. Minimum 7 kilo.

Ter perse : Onze Jongelui.
6 BLOEMRAND. 8

No. 482, corps 32. Minimum 10 kilo.

Facio in den strijd
2 AMSTEL. 5

No. 483, corps 36. Minimum 13 kilo.

Hilversum.
STEM 8

▲ Part of a type specimen of the
Amsterdamsche Lettergieterij (Amsterdam
Type Foundry). 'Bold Egyptienne', late
nineteenth century. Actual size.

▲ Curves with different dynamics: *Coranto, Walbaum, BigVesta, Garamond.*

▲ Nicolas Jenson's letterforms, Eusebius of Caesarea, *De evangelica praeparatione,* 1470, enlarged.
BIBLIOTECA CIVICA VERONA, PHOTO: RICCARDO OLOCCO

3 Type and language

Writing and speaking are both manifestations of language, each with its own properties. What they share is vocabulary, the way sentences are formed, and how discourse is built up. However, speech is transient – it exists only in the here and now, unless recorded, and then it may be hard to retrieve. Writing is much more permanent and functions across time and space. Speakers use intonation, gestures and facial expressions (what linguists call suprasegmental phenomena) for catching and holding attention, with a few signals borrowed from writing such as gestured quotation marks. Written language is usually more clearly organized, with errors removed, and often includes a wider variety of words. Despite such distinctions, there is relatively little difference between spoken and written language when it comes to understanding by listeners and readers.[1]

In addition to the properties of writing already mentioned, written text has its own means for clarification and guidance, such as italic and bold. Early in the seventh century the basic set of signs for written language – the letters – was fundamentally expanded when Isidore of Seville (*c.* 560–636) wrote the *Etymologiae* towards the end of his life, an encyclopedic work, including a chapter on punctuation.[2] Over time this has become a large collection of graphic conventions which directly influence linguistic meaning and clarify texts. It is called the 'grammar of legibility'[a] and was started by scribes: 'A scribe ... had to observe a kind of decorum in his copy in order to ensure that the message of the text was easily understood.'[3] It was adopted by those engaged in typography in the middle of the fifteenth century, then adapted to typographic practice, and has since grown considerably.

Although the concept of the grammar of legibility stems from palaeography, it works effectively for typography and type design. It constitutes a well organized body of features with knowledge about their applications, with both micro- and macro-typographic components, oriented towards readers. These are the

a] Parkes (1992), p 23; Parkes (2008), p 57. This palaeographic instrument, which functions for typography as well, can serve scripts other than the Latin script. The English language includes both 'legibility' and 'readability', and the distinction between them is not entirely clear. In most other languages it is one concept, although Roland Reuß (2014, pp 55–57) suggests that the German terms 'leserlich' and 'lesbar' are roughly equivalent to the English. In his *Letters of Credit* (1986), pp 30, 31, Walter Tracy gives a somewhat complicated explanation for both terms. Simply put though, readability is the domain of authors and editors, legibility that of type designers, typographers and graphic designers.

ingredients that can greatly improve the effectiveness of typeset texts.[b] The core of the contribution by type designers consists of sets of thoughtfully planned letterforms with carefully fixed spaces in and around all characters that enable a regular flow of text, including

b] For type designers and typographers, written language means typeset language. The advantage of the word 'typeset' is that it covers both texts printed on paper and displayed on screens.

italic and variations such as light or bold. The typographer's role includes setting sensible wordspaces, the adjustment of interlinear space to the vertical dimensions of a typeface and to line lengths, and aspects of layout or organization such as making visible structures and hierarchies of text, combining text and images, or the use of space on a larger scale.

An early and important addition to the grammar of legibility was the wordspace, first used by Irish monks around the beginning of the eighth century.[4] Numerals joined letters in the fifteenth century, and early in the sixteenth century small capitals were introduced.[5] Also, during the first half of the sixteenth century, italic was given its present-day role as a secondary script, and bold was added in the course of the nineteenth century.[6] Other elements belonging to the grammar of legibility are the chapter, the paragraph, headlines and subheadings – clues for understanding the organization of a text; also footnotes, tables of contents, and other prelims as well as end matter.

c] Other important and recent publications of this kind are: *Lesetypographie* (1997) by Hans Peter Willberg and Friedrich Forssman; *Detailtypografie* (2002) by Friedrich Forssman and Ralf de Jong; *Type & Typography* (2002) by Phil Baines and Andrew Haslam; *Buchstabenkommenseltenallei n* (2009) by Indra Kupferschmid; *Shaping Text* (2012) by Jan Middendorp; *Die perfekte Lesemachine* (2014) by Roland Reuß; and *Sprachsatz* (2016) by Michael Bundscherer.

In a novel or on many websites hardly more than the most basic ingredients of the grammar are applied, while they can abound in a dictionary or a magazine. All these features are the result of a long and continuous pursuit of clarity and accessibility of text. They have been collected and published, for example as *Hart's Rules for Compositors and Readers* (1992), and *The Elements of Typographic Style* (1996) by Robert Bringhurst (1946–).[c]

d] A glyph is the specific design or form of a character in a typeface. The character 'g' can be designed as **g**, **g** or **g**, and many more variations have been made. Type designers design glyphs. The grammar of legibility has in part been put together as a depiction of typographic signs with a description of their function and usage: *Type design standards* (1996) of the Agfa Corporation, by Elizabeth Smith and Cynthia Hollandsworth (not publicly available).

The contribution by type designers to the grammar of legibility is more than just letterforms and their interior and surrounding spaces; it amounts to collections of glyphs[d] – namely fonts – and, moreover, a well considered group of fonts.[7] Each font contains lowercase characters, capitals, several kinds of figures (for example lining and old style), punctuation marks and diacritics, small capitals, currency symbols, and various other signs. Fonts also contain the characters for several languages and sometimes also for more than one script, such as Cyrillic and Greek combined with Latin.

And fonts are made in many weights, from very light to ultra black, as roman and italic, sometimes condensed and wide, to be used in a broad range of sizes.

Sometimes special versions are made for small and large sizes, and related designs with different details can be combined in a type family: for example, with and without serifs, or with thin and very heavy serifs. Different scripts such as Devanagari and Latin can be treated as stylistically related designs.[e]

The grammar of legibility is by now an integrated group of components to elucidate typeset language – language being the *raison d'être* of type and its design.

e] As far as letters, numerals, and punctuation marks – indeed all the signs in a font – are concerned in the grammar of legibility, all are part of a much larger body of characters: Unicode.

Although the letters of the Latin script are phonetic symbols, they have to represent many different and sometimes vastly divergent sounds, and so they sometimes require additional marks, called diacritics, to represent as well as possible all the languages typeset in the Latin script.[f] The design of alternative character sets more suitable to a particular language has been attempted, by Pierre di Sciullo (1961–), for example, with *le Sintetik* (1992) for French, comprising 16 signs instead of 26.[8] Although it is an interesting and amusing experiment, such an approach ruins the relative universality of the Latin script, with a Babylonian confusion of scripts as a possible result. Although Latin letterforms arbitrarily represent various sounds in many languages, they facilitate reading all these different languages.

f] The present number of languages represented by the Latin script stands at 131. In 2015, the Kazakh government announced that the Latin alphabet would replace Cyrillic as the writing system for the Kazakh language by 2025. – https://en.wikipedia.org/wiki/List_of_languages_by_writing_system#Latin_script (08/04/2017). https://en.wikipedia.org/wiki/Latin_script (08/04/2017).

1. Barton (2007), pp 89–91.
2. Parkes (1992), pp 21–23.
3. Allan (2007), p 87.
4. Parkes (1992), p 23.
5. For numerals see: https://en.wikipedia.org/wiki/Hindu%E2%80%93Arabic_numeral_system (26/09/16); for small caps: Smith (1993), pp 79–106.
6. Twyman (1993), pp 107–142; for italic pp 108–109.
7. See chapter 1, note d.
8. di Sciullo (2006), pp 42–43. http://www.quiresiste.com/projet.php?id_projet=15&lang=fr&id_gabarit=0 (14/09/2017).

▶ Page of 'De Notis Sententiarum', a chapter from: Isidore of Seville, *Libri Etymologiarum*, I, XXI, early eighth century, Weissenburg ms, f. 13v. An early version of the grammar of legibility, written in Northern Italy, 27.3 × 20.9 cm.
HERZOG AUGUST BIBLIOTHEK WOLFENBÜTTEL

▶▶ Bold type (Clarendon) used for key words in text. 158 × 165 mm.
Detail from: K. Baedeker, *Paris and Environs*, 1888, Karl Baedeker.
COLLECTION OF MICHAEL TWYMAN

ad ea uitia : ita q̄ ful ui confodere
fa;it caelum grece · obalar dicitur
Obalur subgeticus eidem ponitur
in hir de quibz dubitatur · utrum tolli
debeat nec ne fr̄ poni

Lymnircus · id ē uirgula cū duabz
geminis punctis · ea ut̄ opponitur
in hir locir que aliq̄ ratione reddūtur
in asspectu eodem iterū redditur
rationibz ctaliter allatur

Antigrafur cū puncto · ad ponitur
ubi in translationibz diuersa uel uitiur
habetur

Aragus cū obolo ħ ubi super uacua
ap̄ uitur · ad eadem in hir ut̄ uerbir
qui non in ueloso positi ā uel

Paragrafur ponit̄ ad seq̄nti
dur p̄ upoib; que in congestiõe
tēnur̄ quemadmodū lucis ad loco
loca allocir · ex q̄; non̄ex q̄r õnibz
in ut̄ gongr̄t̄iõe appōnit̄ · ac cū ut̄
mini ut diuer̄ sir ut̄ sententiis
sequentur

Positura ē p̄ uersu · q̄ ut̄ grafo
contraria · et ideo sic ē appōnit̄ quia
sicut ille prin̄ q̄ū uox ē lectur̄
finir ut̄ prin̄ significat require

UC nt̄ grec̄ utliḡ gur̄ in hir gr̄t̄ inim
puncto

Positio in hir locī ubi que lḡe durat · ad obter̄
se q̄ uel uoluim in pōct̄uā
Astrismus ponit̄ ad eo ut̄ uersu q̄
ordo ḡ grec̄ mutadur ut̄ sic et in hir a quiuera
positiam in ut̄ enmur̄

Astrismus cū punctato q̄ oi uer̄ in hir
ubi inter eadem unera dupliciter ut̄ uer̄ uel c̄
bicul̄ qui poq̄r eth q̄n dur̄ sic

Diple ut̄ ut̄ q̄ grec̄ nos sic de ponit̄ uel
ecclesiar q̄re intrap̄ ut̄ atq̄ uit̄ uel
dem̄ prophetar̄ de sermonia significatur̄

Diple p̄ grecos ut̄ hic p̄ uers̄ super uer̄ sit
posuit · oms ḡ uer̄ cibz ad p̄ q̄n da p̄
T olympi · ut̄ celo

Diple p̄ grā mine · lllac cū geminis
q̄ ut̄ hic cū q̄q̄r in hir apponebant qu
q̄ ad dicit̄ q̄r prin̄ non p̄ uer̄ ut̄ dic
iua ad de ut̄ act̄ ut̄ q̄r mut̄ ut̄ uer̄

In hir de uer̄ q̄ ut̄ ut̄ uir̄ andis

Diple obelismen e lunar ponit̄ ad q̄n
In cō medur̄ ut̄ traa grece ut̄ p̄ q̄ ut̄

Altera obolus min̄ie q̄ q̄q̄r c̄ proph̄
et h̄ q̄ oph̄ur in ffen̄ dur̄

Adulterū cū obolo ut̄ de ut̄ ponit̄ ut̄
ad ul; quid p̄ p̄ ficiunt ut̄ uer̄ in uer̄ bir

Nt̄ ut̄ ut̄ ḡ se fundo contin̄ur · nor̄ h̄ mini
quid p̄qr ut̄ c̄ uer̄ obl̄acta

Diple p̄ subḡ obl̄i cū ponit̄ ut̄ ad condi
lol̄ ope ut̄ dem̄ por̄ uru
p̄ sonarū q̄ mouta

scènes des deuxièmes and stalles d'orchestre 4 ; stalles des troisièmes 2½ fr. Ladies not admitted to the orchestra places.

Bouffes Parisiens (Pl. R, 21 ; *II*), a small theatre in the Passage Choiseul near the Italian Opera, the specialty of which is comic operettas and parodies. It was established by Offenbach in 1855. — Avant-scènes 10 ; fauteuils d'orchestre 6 fr. — Ladies not admitted to the orchestra stalls.

Théâtre de la Porte St. Martin (Pl. R, 24 ; *III*), in the Boulevard St. Martin, burned down by the Communists in May, 1871, but since rebuilt. Dramas and spectacular pieces are performed here. — Avant-scènes 14 ; fauteuils d'orchestre 9 ; stalles d'orchestre 5 ; stalles des troisièmes de face 2½ fr.

Théâtre de la Renaissance (Pl. R, 24 ; *III*), next door to the preceding. Modern comedies. — Avant-scènes 12 ; fauteuils d'orchestre 7 ; stalles d'orchestre 4 ; stalles de deuxième galerie 2 fr.

Théâtre du Châtelet, Place du Châtelet (Pl. R, 24 ; *V*), a very roomy edifice, specially fitted up for fairy scenes and ballet, lighted by a large reflector in the roof, which can be removed in summer for ventilation. — Fauteuils de balcon de premier rang 8 ; fauteuils d'orchestre and loges 7 ; stalles d'orchestre 5 ; pourtour 4 ; parterre 2½ ; deuxième amphithéâtre 1½ fr.

Théâtre de la Gaîté (Pl. R, 24 ; *III*), Square des Arts et Métiers. It has several times changed its name and its specialty; at present spectacular pieces and operettas are given. — Avant-scènes 10 ; fauteuils d'orchestre 7 ; stalles d'orchestre 4 ; stalles de la seconde galerie 3 ; stalles de la troisième galerie 2½ and 2 fr.

Théâtre des Nouveautés (Pl. R, 21), Boulevard des Italiens 28. Vaudevilles and operettas. — Avant-scènes 15 ; fauteuils d'orchestre 8 and 7 ; stalles d'orchestre 5 fr. Ladies not admitted to the orchestra places.

Ambigu - Comique (Pl. R, 24 ; *III*), Boulevard St. Martin 2 ; dramas, melodramas, and 'patriotic' pieces. — Avant-scènes 10 ; fauteuils d'orchestre 6 ; fauteuils et loges de foyer 4 and 3 ; stalles de galerie 2½ and 2 fr.

Folies Dramatiques (Pl. R, 27 ; *III*), Boulevard St. Martin, or rather Rue de Bondy 40, near the Place de la République. Operettas, etc. Seats for 1600. — Avant-scènes and loges de balcon de face 8 ; fauteuils d'orchestre 6 ; stalles de balcon 2 fr.

Eden Théâtre (Pl. R, 18 ; *II*), Rue Boudreau, for pantomimes and ballets, which are, however, about to yield to another class of representations.

Among the best of the other theatres are the following : —

Théâtre de Cluny, Boul. St. Germain 71, near the Musée de Cluny, the 'Gymnase' of the left bank (seats 6 fr. to 1¼ fr.). — *Château d'Eau,* at one time the '*Opéra Populaire*', Rue de Malte 50, near the Place de la République, for popular dramas (5 fr. to 50 c.). — *Théâtre Beaumarchais* or *Fantaisies Parisiennes*, Boul.

Hindi poets of the 20th century मुक्तिबोध का जन्म श्यौपुर ग्वालियर में हुआ। नागपुर विश्वविद्यालय से हिन्दी में एम॰ए॰ (Master of Arts) की उपाधि ली तथा आजीवन पत्रकारिता से जुड़े रहे। Journalistic and literary career मुक्तिबोध अपनी लम्बी कविताओं के लिए प्रसिध्द हैं। इनकी कविता में जीवन के प्रति विषाद और आक्रोश है। Principal works include 'चांद का मुंह टेढा है' तथा 'भूरी-भूरी खाक धूल', 'मुक्तिबोध रचनावली' (6-खण्ड) में प्रकाशित हुई है। (September 1964) He had been one of the most prominent Hindi poets, essayist, literary and political critic, and fiction writers of the 20th century. He is widely considered one of the pioneers of प्रयोगवादी कविता (experimental poetry) movement in literature.

On n'e þa serieu, kan on a di-sed an.
- Un þo soir, foin de þok e de la limonade,
de kafe daþageur so lusdre sekladan?
- On va sou le diieul ver de la þronnade.

le diieul sande þon dan le þon soir de guin?
l'er e þarfoi si dou k'on fern la þoþiere;
le van ç'arge de þrui, - la vile n'e þas loin, -
a de þarfin de vigne e de þarfin de þiere...

▲ Vaibhav Singh, 2011, *Eczar*, Devanagari with related Latin. MA Typeface Design of the University of Reading.

▲ Pierre di Sciullo, *le Sintétik*, 1992.

On n'est pas sérieux, quand on a dix-sept ans.
– Un beau soir, foin des bocks et de la limonade,
Des cafés tapageurs aux lustres éclatants!
– On va sous les tilleuls verts de la promenade.

Les tilleuls sentent bon dans les bons soirs de juin!
L'air est parfois si doux qu'on ferme la paupière;
le vent chargé de bruits, – la ville n'est pas loin, –
A des parfums de vigne et des parfums de bière …

4 History

The many historical typefaces which will be discussed in this theory [see for example chapters 5 and 7] attest to the influence that the typographic past and historical letterforms have had on twentieth-century type design, and still exert on the profession. A vast amount of literature covers the history of typography and type design, although there are still areas to explore or earlier studies needing revision.[a] Part of this history is the degeneration in the course of the nineteenth century of typefaces based on the ideas of the Didots and Bodoni (1740–1813).

a] For example, the work of some early printers of the fifteenth century is reexamined with much better photography than ever before by Riccardo Olocco.

As a class or theme, the descendants of the Didots' and Bodoni's type designs are named 'modern face', while earlier designs are labelled 'old face' [see chapter 7].[b] Both show a difference between thick and thin parts, in old face at an angle of approximately 30–45°, and in modern face strictly vertical-horizontal. In his theory of writing Gerrit Noordzij (1931–) has called these effects 'translation' and 'expansion', the first the outcome of moving a broad-nibbed pen at a more or less fixed angle in relation to the writing line or baseline, and the second of applying pressure, spreading a pointed and flexible nib, with widening strokes as a consequence.[c]

b] Often, instead of 'old face' and 'modern face', the terms 'old style' and 'modern style' are used. Although not wrong, the latter terminology is confusing because *Old Style* is the name of a British type design from 1860 (see chapter 16, note c), which remained common until the early twentieth century, also in America.

c] Noordzij (1985), p 5. For historical examples see Osley (1972), pp 100, 107. The pointed and flexible pen was probably used first between 1570 and 1580 by Ludovico Curione. His predecessor Giovan Francesco Cresci used a pointed but inflexible pen.

Those modern faces used for body copy in books, magazines, newspapers, and advertisements had become during the nineteenth century 'crawling masses of heavy parallel lines',[1] at least on the European continent. In England and the United States the modern face remained more open and was treated less dogmatically, for example with what in America were called Scotch faces.[2]

Meanwhile 'fat faces' were developed and an incredible variety of decorative letterforms came onto the market. From about 1840 several attempts were made to replace the decadent modern text faces, for example with a return to Caslon's types.[3] By the twentieth century there were various initiatives to improve the form of type (often by looking back in time): for instance, the accumulation of historical knowledge by T.B. Reed (1852–1893) and D.B. Updike (1860–1941), and the 'Garamond' revival.[4] One great stimulus was the work of William Morris (1834–1896) at his Kelmscott Press (1891–8), and the ensuing rebirth of calligraphy, which was largely due to Edward Johnston (1872–1944).[5] His calligraphic work is rooted in writing with the broad-nibbed pen, a position many calligraphers maintain into the twenty-first century. Gerrit Noordzij stated in 1982: 'We may write with many different tools but western writing will always evoke shapes that have been defined by the western tool: the broad nibbed pen.'[6] However, as mentioned above, Noordzij does acknowledge the pointed and flexible pen in his theory of writing.

In the last quarter of the twentieth century the interest in writing with a broad-nibbed pen declined, and it was dropped from the curriculum of many art schools and similar institutions internationally – at least with regard to the Latin script. Simultaneously the attitude towards the history of typography and type design shifted, and criticism arose of modernist graphic design, typography, and type design (as practised from the late 1950s in the Western world) as being too rigid and uniform. After the turn of the twenty-first century, the aversion to Modernism subsided and its history was given attention again.[7] Calligraphy has recovered, especially as part of lettering, and has returned to education.[8] The interest in the general history of typography and type design has never been absent and is by now so firmly embedded in type-design education that in educational programmes it is hardly mentioned as a separate subject.[9]

Meanwhile, with almost thirty years of the web for daily company and nearly two decades into the twenty-first century, type design is a profession with goals far beyond printed paper – the traditional territory of the history of typography and type design. Still, anyone embarking on a study of type design has around fifteen years of experience in reading, and has for that time been exposed to typographic conventions with an extensive history and often to letterforms connected to ancient models. Whether they want it or not, when type designers begin their professional lives, this luggage accompanies them to their assigned tasks, many of which are now screen-based. In the company of well-known letterforms and their users, the history of type on paper has spread to screens.

The reverse is also happening: conventions that have become specific to typography on screen show up on paper. Typography on screen has a background in word processing, which in turn has a background in office typography with typewriters. In typed letters it was the custom to use a full blank line to indicate the beginning of a new paragraph – that is now *the* indication of a new paragraph on screen. This is a change in the grammar of legibility [see chapter 3], which has migrated from screen to paper, beginning to replace the printed tradition of using an indent to mark a new paragraph. The more recent use of colour on screen is also appearing on paper, for example with text in light blue, whereas typography has for a long time been mainly black and monochrome. The use of sanserifs for body text is widespread on screen and increasing on paper.

A benefit of knowing about the history of type design is the possibility to build on the past, to chart developments from past to present, and to extend these into the future. This can be done by staying close to ancient historical models or to more recent examples, or by striving for maximum originality within all the conditions entailed by type design, many of which have a long history. The originality of a type design can only be measured through comparison with earlier ones, and, of course, with contemporary designs.

1. Ovink (1971a), p 18.
2. De Vinne (1900), p 212.
3. Johnson (1959), pp 80–91.
4. For the accumulation of historical knowledge see: Morison (1963), pp xxi–xxiv; for the Garamond revival see: Beaujon (1926), pp 131–179.
5. Clayton (2013), pp 270–278.
6. Noordzij (1982), p 8; Clayton (2013), p 115.
7. Naegele (2012), *passim*.
8. Flor (2016), pp 51–63; Van Blokland (2015), pp 228–232; Barmettler (2016), p 401.
9. http://typefacedesign.net/courses/matd/ (02/03/2017).

A HISTORY OF THE OLD ENGLISH LETTER FOUNDRIES

With Notes

Historical and Bibliographical

on the Rise and Progress of English Typography

by

TALBOT BAINES REED

A new edition revised and enlarged by

A. F. JOHNSON

FABER AND FABER LIMITED

24 Russell Square, London

▲ *A History of the Old English Letter Foundries* by T.B. Reed, 1, originally published in 1887. This revised and expanded edition is from 1952. 27.4 × 18.5 cm.

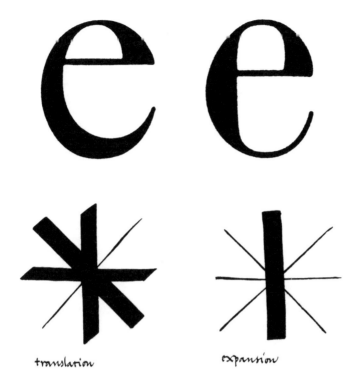

translation   expansion

Parmi cette immense multitude de divers animaux, aucun
ne borne à lui-même son amour, on voit un sexe désirer
l'autre ardemment, leur feu commun les réunit tous deux, le
plaisir continue ordinairement après leur union, ils s'aiment
encore tendrement dans leur race, la mère nourrit ses petits et le père les veille constamment. Ces chers nourrissons
commencent-ils à connoître leurs forces, leur instinct se re-

ABCDEFGHIJKLMNOPQRSTUVWXYZ

ABCDEFGHIJKLMNOPQRSTUVWXYZ

⬀ Old face: *Caslon*, left; and modern face:
Bodoni, right.

▲ Translation and expansion. Actual size.
From: Gerrit Noordzij, *The Stroke of the Pen*, 1982,
Koninklijke Academie van Beeldende Kunsten.

▲ Crawling mass of heavy parallel lines, as
G.W. Ovink described this style of type.
Actual size.
From: Walter Wilkes, *Atlas zur Geschichte der Schrift*,
1986, Technische Hochschule Darmstadt, 'Grobe
Cicero' reproduced from the type specimen of the
Decker typefoundry, 1862, Berlin.

▶ *Scotch-face* of James Conner's Sons' foundry. Made in the nineteenth century, after 1861. Actual size.
From: Theodore Low De Vinne, *Plain Printing Types*, 1900.

▼ *Caslon*, cast from matrices made with the original punches. Actual size.
From: Specimen of H.W. Caslon & Co Ltd, 1924.

▼ Full, blank lines to indicate the beginning of new paragraphs on screen, instead of an indent, as is the custom in many printed texts.
Part of the website of *The Guardian* (15/04/2018).

HORACE GREELEY was born in Amherst, New Hampshire, 3d February, 1811, and died in Pleasantville, Westchester County, New York, 29th November, 1872. His earliest training as a printer began in East Poultney, Vermont, in 1825. In 1831 he went to New York. In 1833 he began as a master printer; in 1834 he established the "New Yorker," in 1840 the "Log Cabin," and in 1841 the "New York Tribune," which, during his long term of editorship, became a journal of unprecedented influence in politics. He was a clear thinker, and a ready writer in a style of remarkable strength. A fearless opponent of slavery he made many enemies, but all hostilities ended with his death. By general consent he takes a rightful place in the annals of typography as "our later Franklin."

HILE the City of London declined to license a place for theatrical performances within its limits, the Stationers' Company was to some extent redressing the grievance by registering for publication the popular drama of the day; and over and above all there was the eminently favourable attitude of the Court and the nobles towards the theatre and dramatic art.

From the year 1554 to the present day, with a gap of five years from 1571 to 1576, the Registers of the Stationers' Company are intact. For our present purpose, we are mainly concerned with the volumes containing early entries of the plays of William Shakespeare. Thanks to the late Professor Arber's labours these volumes are available in an excellent

Cos creative director Karin Gustafsson, who launched the Milan project seven years ago, is known for offering artists creative carte blanche. "It's about sharing a creator that we believe in, someone exciting for others to know about," she says. "Phillip is someone we've been watching who always has an interesting dialogue with his surroundings."

Those surroundings have been mostly Los Angeles and Palm Springs, where Smith was raised by his property developer father and interior designer mother. "I grew up walking through homes that were being wood-framed, so always had a sense of a structure evolving, but my mom's work meant she honed my eye towards colour."

Having studied architecture at Rhode Island School of Design, Smith decided it wasn't for him. "I couldn't do what I'm doing without my architectural education, but what I'm doing is not architecture. I'm still interested in terms of its root qualities: space, light, time and creating art at the scale of architecture."

5 Norms

In *An Essay on Typography* (1931) Eric Gill (1882–1940) wrote: 'as there is a norm of letter form – the bare body so to say, of letters – there is also a norm of letter clothes'. He added that the 'first notable attempt to work out the norm for plain letters' was Edward Johnston's sanserif for the London Underground (1916), which he suggests was perhaps improved by his own *Gill Sans* (1928).[1] He also mentions a classical model: 'we have inherited an alphabet of such pre-eminent rationality and dignity as the Roman'.[2] Roman capitals, especially those of the inscription on the Trajan column in Rome, have been very influential during the twentieth century: they have defined what capitals should look like for several generations of designers.[a]

a] Mosley (1964), pp 17–48; Shaw (2015), *passim*. The first photographic reproduction of the Trajan inscription publicly available was included in Edward Johnston's *Writing & Illuminating, and Lettering* (1906).

For both capitals and lowercase the work of the French punchcutter Claude Garamond (*c.* 1480–1561) has been proposed as exemplary. Jan Tschichold (1902–1974), the famous modernist and modern classicist,[b] was exceptionally enthusiastic about his work: 'His old face design is ... the culmination of a two-thousand-year-long development. ... the Renaissance roman, which was given its definitive and unsurpassable form by Claude Garamond.'[c] Tschichold's admiration for Garamond is also expressed in his type design *Sabon*, published in 1967.[3] Previously, around the beginning of the twentieth century, the roman type of Nicolas Jenson (originally made shortly after 1470) had been favoured as a model, soon followed by the types made by Francesco Griffo (1450–1518) for Aldus Manutius (1449–1515), and by Garamond's letters. The importance of Garamond for twentieth-century type design is evident from the more than thirty variations based on his work (and on types cut by later colleagues) made available between 1898 and the present.[4]

b] McLean (1975), *passim*. Before Tschichold became a modern classicist he was a militant modernist.

c] Tschichold, 'Die Bedeutung der Tradition für den Entwurf neuer Schriften' (1992, vol.2), p 336. This text was originally published in 1966. Along with Garamond's romans Tschichold admired equally the italics of Robert Granjon.

But do the Trajan capitals plus Garamond's lowercase make a norm? For some time and for some genres of publication they did – and still do.[d] Jan Tschichold was for much of the second part of his career a book designer, which determined his view.[5] Another ardent

d] Barton (2007), pp 73–76. For different kinds of printed texts or of written communication 'genre' is often used, while for different ways of speaking 'register' is a common term. Since the conventions of written and spoken language are blended in screen-based communication or computer-mediated communication (CMC), 'register' is also applied to fields of written communication.

book lover was Stanley Morison (1889–1967), the spiritual father of *Times New Roman* (1932). Advising typographers on the choice of typeface in his *First Principles of Typography* (1930), he hinted at the existence of a norm: '... the more often he is going to use it, the more closely its design must approximate to the general idea held in the mind of the reader'.[6] It is plausible that this general idea corresponds with Gill's norms.

To stay with books for a moment, with literary books (particularly novels), the majority if not all of these are set in one size of one typeface, usually a well-known and seriffed one, corresponding with Morison's advice, with chapter headings often in a larger size of the same face. The exteriors, on the other hand, the covers or dust jackets, often show a different world: colourful, illustrated, sometimes with text in striking and less conventional typefaces than found inside the books, or with conventional letterforms in unusual arrangements or so enlarged that distinctive features of the letterforms become visible [see chapter 17]. These exteriors and interiors are intended for the same readership. Using books, most readers seem to be able to handle conventional and less conventional typefaces nearly simultaneously.

There are, however, major differences between the covers and the interiors of literary books: texts on the outsides are mostly short and set in large sizes and are much more often subject to changes for stylistic reasons than typefaces for the interiors set in small sizes. When Morison wrote the text quoted above, he was clearly thinking of the insides of books. Typographers' choices for this application change so slowly that the semblance of a norm easily aris-

e] To take just one example, *Career of Evil* by Robert Galbraith (a pseudonym of Harry Potter's creator J.K. Rowling) was published in 2015, typeset in *Bembo* (1929), a typeface then 86 years old.

es.[e] In general the following applies: the longer the text, the more conventional the choice of typeface usually is, and vice versa: the shorter the text the less conventional typefaces can be. This is possible because a text of a few words is read very quickly, in a fraction of a second, and offers ample time to be viewed and interpreted [see chapter 17].

Also, the smaller the readership, the more unconventional typefaces can be, especially for specific readers, such as the patrons of a gallery with experimental art, or the students of an art school who may design radically innovative letterforms, mostly for their own use. The larger the readership, the less inclined typographers are to make unusual choices; then they opt for conventional type designs, as in newspapers. Large quantities of text are read differently than a few words, with more concentration on the content and its mental reconstruction and understanding.

Adrian Frutiger (1928–2015) made a well-known attempt to visualize the general idea of a letterform by superimposing some of his designs to arrive at a shape that all his typefaces have in common, and which

f] Osterer (2008), pp 410, 411. Frutiger has also superimposed other typefaces, one of which is *Garamond*, but less convincingly than with his own designs. See: Frutiger (1980), p 64.

shows the effect of one mind and one hand on the different designs.[f] Frutiger has said in connection with this exercise: 'The core of the character is as a pure tone in music, while the outer form causes the actual sound.'[7] This is reminiscent of Gill's body and clothes.

With this shape Adrian Frutiger visualized his norm or average (for a letter **a**) and probably he is not far from a more general norm, but this is not a shape that functions for all kinds of type designs. To achieve that we would have to repeat Frutiger's exercise on a much larger scale with the work of many designers and over a number of years. With text faces you would then plausibly see a somewhat less personal average than Frutiger's and you would see it change slowly, very slowly. For display faces you would get in all probability several norms, much more prone to change through time.

Edward Johnston wrote: 'essential or structural forms are the simplest forms which preserve the characteristic structure, distinctiveness, and proportions of each individual letter'; and: 'The "Essential forms" may be briefly defined as the necessary parts.' What he shows are skeletons.[8] In the 1920s Bauhaus modernists promoted geometric construction as a method for establishing the essence of letterforms, but Frutiger's core shape, wherein details can still be detected, seems to be more convincing as an average than skeletal forms without any details or purely geometric shapes.

The use of type by typographers, graphic designers, publishers and now also by many non-professionals – readers with a knowledge of type and typography acquired through working with devices offering a choice of typefaces – can be represented as a kind of stellar cloud, dense at the centre and thinning towards the periphery.[9] It includes all typefaces in use at any point in time – for instance right now. At the centre, close together, are many well-known and widely used typefaces, all with comparable qualities, clear and sensible designs, with and without serifs and of sound and equal legibility.[h] These are truly conventional typefaces with very familiar details, moving slowly through time – many are of a venerable age, but recent designs can be found here as well.

Occasionally an old one shuffles out of the nebula. The farther out you go to the vague edge of this typographic stellar cloud, the more unusual letterforms are and the less they are used. They may attract attention on publication, but many will have a short practical life and fade away soon. This happened to many of the experimental type designs made between 1990 and 2000, which was a period when numerous unconventional typefaces were designed.

g] This cloud-image was used for the first time in a lecture by Gerry Leonidas in November 2014 for the MA Typeface Design at the Department of Typography & Graphic Communication, University of Reading, UK.

h] Beier (2012), pp 124–130. Studies comparing the legibility of typefaces with and without serifs have never led to a final conclusion. Meanwhile the use of sanserifs for texts of some length set in small sizes has increased, and the legibility of both kinds of typefaces now seems to be equal.

Near the edge of the type cloud surprises can be found with unexpected combinations of design features, as in *Bosozoku* (2015) designed by Thibault Baralon (1993–), influenced by shapes of custom cars built by members of a Japanese subculture. The cars feature wide and flat additions (a kind of spoilers), wind pipes, and more. It is surprising and unexpected that this typeface is reasonably legible.[9]

Ideal or perfect letterforms do not exist; that was a concept of both the Renaissance and Modernism. Letterforms (mostly capitals) were subjected to geometric construction, for example by Felice Feliciano (1433–1479) in 1463, Luca Pacioli (1445–1517) in 1509, and Albrecht Dürer (1471–1528) in 1525.[10] In the twentieth century Josef Albers (1888–1976) and Herbert Bayer (1900–1985) pursued ideal letterforms with geometry as a basis.[11] The letterforms cut by Garamond and colleagues seemed to be ideal according to Tschichold and many other typographers, but you only need to look at the thirty-odd renewed versions – published by the American Type Founders (1918), Monotype (1923), Stempel (1925), International Typeface Corporation (1975), Adobe (1989, 2005) and other firms – to see how widely such a concept can be interpreted. Which one is the ideal version?

Any of these Garamond variations – together coming close to a norm – and a design like *White no sugar* (1997) – made from plastic coffee cup stirrers by Anna-Lisa Schönecker (1967–)[12] – are very far apart. These disparate designs cannot be made to fit the same norm: *White no sugar* is positioned in the type cloud at quite a distance from the centre, although its letterforms are not too difficult to recognize. And what about script typefaces, many of which are rather extravagant, though not as whimsical as *White no sugar*? Italics certainly have their own norm, probably more than one: italic capitals are more or less slanted versions of roman capitals but the lowercase shows some fundamental differences with roman lowercase, notably in the *a*, *e* and *g*. These letterforms can be found in upright type designs as well: the *g*, for instance, has figured in sanserifs since the nineteenth century (such as *Akzidenz Grotesk*, 1898).

Yet another norm is behind the refined geometric letterforms of *Futura* (1927) by Paul Renner (1878–1956) – with one qualification: the proportions of the capitals of *Futura* are purely classical, with its slender **B**, **E** and **S**, and wide **M**, **O** and **Q**.[13] The reappearance here of a Roman model suggests that, though not an ideal, this is a norm too, while the lowercase of *Futura* adheres to a geometric norm. It is obvious that no single norm is at work in type design but several can be distinguished, and they can be mixed.

....

1. Gill (1954), pp 48–49.
2. Gill (1954), p 28.
3. McLean (1975), pp 114, 115.
4. Beaujon (1926), *passim*; Falk (1975), pp 40, 41.

5. McLean (1975), *passim.* Tschichold's appreciation of *Garamond* was, however, already apparent in his modernist phase: see Burke (2007), p 149 n4, pp 181 & 198.
6. Morison (1930), p 62.
7. Osterer (2008), p 438.
8. Johnston (1962, first published 1906), pp 204, 239, 240.
9. Filser (2016), pp 34, 35.
10. Mosley (1964), p 34.
11. Fleischmann (1984), pp 259, 278, 279.
12. Brody (2012), pp 314, 315.
13. Burke (1998a), pp 95, 96.

ABCDEFGHIJKL
MNOPQRSTUV
WWXYZ&QU
abcdefghijklmn
opqrstuvwxyz
£1234567890
.,:;?!()'' "" !*/

▲ Edward Johnston's sanserif, 1916, London
Transport.
From: Justin Howes, *Johnston's Underground Type,*
2000, Capital Transport.

45

improve
enhance
get better
recuperate
shape up

Deity is the unsurpassable form
by this very form in a subseque
the creatures are instances of s
of creativity. Every actuality, d
is both creature and creator in
The creator is the eminent or u
of creative-created actuality.

ABCDEFGHIKL
MNOPQ RSTV
XYZabcdefghil
mnopqrsſtuvxyz
1234567890 ,. ' !?;:- ⁹ ꝰ

rpassable only

hase) of creativity;

ssable forms

e or otherwise,

ion to others.

passable form

► *Gill Sans*, 1928, Monotype.

▲ Claude Garamond's Gros Canon,
c. 1549. Actual size.
From: Harry Carter, *A View of Early Typography*,
1969, Oxford University Press.

◄ *Sabon*, 1967, Stempel / Monotype /
Linotype.

potero) ‚q̈ potero ‚ diligent
’. Immo Hercle fiat potii
fi facere ipfe ‚ ne fiat ‚ potes
impedio : illud autem idec
|uia te putabam ánte‚q̈ iftu

THE SMALL HOUSE AT ALLINGTON   151

father to son, and from uncle to nephew, and, in one
instance, from second cousin to second cousin, the
sceptre had descended in the family of the Dales; and
the acres had remained intact, growing in value and not
decreasing in number, though guarded by no entail and
protected by no wonderful amount of prudence or wis-
dom. The estate of Dale of Allington had been coter-
minous with the parish of Allington for some hundreds
of years; and though, as I have said, the race of squires
had possessed nothing of superhuman discretion and
had perhaps been guided in their walks through life by
no very distinct principles, still there had been with them
so much of adherence to a sacred law, that no acre of the
property had ever been parted from the hands of the

▲ Typeface cut by Francesco Griffo for
Aldus Manutius, c. 1495. Enlarged.
From: Pietro Bembo, *De Aetna*, 1495/96.
BIBLIOTECA PALATINA PARMA
PHOTO: RICCARDO OLOCCO

▶ The Dutch translation by Jan van Krimpen
of Stanley Morison's *First Principles of
Typography*. 20.8 × 13 cm.
Stanley Morison, *Grondbeginselen van de typografie*,
1951, W. de Haan. Bought by Gerard Unger in 1959.

▲ *Times New Roman*, 1932, Monotype.
From: 1962, *The Western Type Book*, 1962,
Hamish Hamilton.

STANLEY MORISON
GRONDBEGINSELEN
VAN DE
TYPOGRAFIE

UITGEVERSMAATSCHAPPIJ
W. DE HAAN N.V. ⁄ UTRECHT

the bottle at room temperature for an hour or so. But if you need to warm it in a hurry, you could nurse the bottle and try to transmit your body heat, or pour its contents into a clean jug or decanter that has been rinsed with hot water and then swirl it around a bit. Or, even more effective, you could pour the wine into a glass and then warm the glass in your hands.

Once you have got your bottle to the right temperature, in hot weather, or in hot rooms, it can be very helpful to keep the opened bottle in one of those vacuum bottle coolers designed to maintain temperatures.

When to open the bottle–and whether to decant
For many people, opening a bottle of wine is a religious sacrament. They have evolved arcane rules about how long different sorts of wine need to 'breathe' before being served. Like many wine scientists, I am sceptical that much can happen to the contents of a bottle of wine via the small surface area in a bottleneck, but it is certainly true that exposure to air can have a massive effect on a wine. Too much aeration of a really old, frail wine can destroy it. On the other hand, judicious aeration of a young wine can mimic the ageing process to a certain extent. For instance, a very tannic, astringent young red, and even a tight, introvert, uncommunicative young white (particularly white burgundy), can seem much more approachable after being exposed to air for an hour or two, or even longer for some young reds such as Barolo and some very smart red bordeaux in which tannins and perfumes play an important part. The most effective way of exposing such wines to air is to decant them. The word 'decant' may sound rather pompous and off-putting, but all it involves is pouring the contents of the wine from the bottle into a clean container–ideally made of neutral glass. A glass jug would do, but

60

▲ Double page with plain text.
Typefaces: *Swift* and *Helvetica*.
18.1 × 22.2 cm.
From: Jancis Robinson, *The 24-hour Wine Expert*, 2016, Penguin Books.

wine decanters have generally been designed to hold the contents of a 75 cl bottle in such a way that the surface area of the wine is big enough to allow lots of interaction between the wine and air. You can even find special decanters for magnums, which are double-size bottles containing 150 cl of wine. In my experience, junk shops are awash with often relatively inexpensive decanters. Pouring the wine vigorously into the decanter helps to aerate it (as does simply swirling any wine poured into a glass).

Another reason for decanting is to separate the wine from any sediment that may have formed in it, as it not only looks rather unappetising, it can taste bitter. An inexpensive wine that has been aggressively clarified before bottling (by filtration, for example) is highly unlikely to have any deposit in the bottle. But as the various compounds in less industrial wine, particularly tannins and pigments, interact with each other, they precipitate sediment, which can sometimes stick to the inside of the bottle but usually falls to the bottom of an upright bottle. To separate the wine from this sediment most effectively it helps to stand the bottle upright for an hour or so and then pour the wine off the sediment against a bright light, either a carefully placed candle or a strong light source.

If you are planning to serve several wines and want to minimize the likelihood of confusion, you could do what's called 'double decanting'. This involves pouring the wine off any deposit into a jug, rinsing the bottle carefully and pouring the sediment-free wine back into the clean bottle, exposing it to as much air as possible along the way.

Wine leftovers

Because prolonged exposure to air – more than a week or so – can rob even young wines of their fruit, it makes sense to keep leftover wine in contact with as little air as possible,

61

RED, WHITE ROSÉ,
FIZZY, SCREWCAP v CORK
WINE MYTHS, OVERPRICED WINES
BOTTLES AS GIFTS, HOW TO CHOOSE
THE 24-HOUR DECODING LABELS
CROWD PLEASERS, WINE EXPERT
By the most respected wine
JANCIS critic in the world
OLD v NEW WORLD, ROBINSON
DECANTING, THE TASTING RITUAL
MATCHING FOOD AND WINE

8-11 FEBRUARY
ART
ROTTERDAM
2018
VAN NELLE
FABRIEK

◀ Hand-lettered cover, a different world from the interior of this book. Design: gray318. 18.1 × 11.1 cm.
From: Jancis Robinson, *The 24-hour Wine Expert*, 2016, Penguin Books.

▲ Unusual letterforms for art lovers. Part of a poster for Art Rotterdam. Logo design: Maarten Evenhuis, 2005.

ABCDEFGHIK
LMNOPQRST
VXYZ·JUW later + forms

Square Capitals.

ƌɛhmu ƞↄↄↄ + late forms +

Round Capitals.

aabcdefghiklm
nopqrstuvxyz { J w w + 3

Small Letters.

A rough Diagram of the structural or "ESSENTIAL FORMS" of the three main types of Letters.

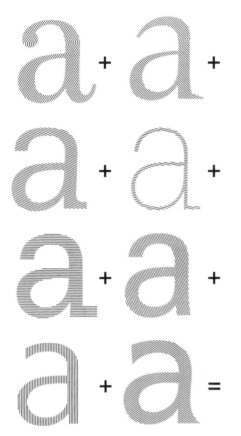

abcdefqhijklm
nopqrstuvwx

◀ Edward Johnston's 'Essential forms', c. 1906.
Enlarged.
From: Edward Johnston, *Writing & Illuminating, and
Lettering*, 1962, Pitman.

▲ Superimposed type designs by Adrian
Frutiger, c. 1980: *Iridium, Meridien,
Egyptienne F, Glypha, Serifa, Univers,
Frutiger, Icone*.
From: Adrian Frutiger, *Type Sign Symbol*, 1980,
abcVerlag.

▲ Geometric letterforms by Herbert Bayer,
1926.
From: Ellen Lupton and J. Abbott Miller, Type Writing,
Emigre Nr. 15, 1990, Emigre.

▲ A visualization of the type cloud, with probable positions of some typefaces.

Eloise came through the door with a bang. WHERES Marty? she cried, a hint of desperation in her tremulous voice. Aw, babe, what's ya want wit' dat creep? He's a Washout Plain and Thin said OSKAR. Now I'm the one who's so full of LOVE and DEVOTiON baby doll. Whaddya say youse and me go an' have ourselves a little violation? Oh Oskar, give it up. You aint nuttin' but a Hack who makes CheapSignage and smokes too much Nicotine. I'd rather have a Hard Tack than ever get stuck wit' you, ya Thickhead. Just then she discovered a Love Letter in the Typewriter. Well Filet my soul she cried. Isn't this Wooly Bully? But Oskar grabbed the love letter and ScrumBled it all up! Hey baby he said dont let this Gen X Crumble get to yer heart with such a cheap DEVICE as a love letter. When he saw the look in her eye, Oskar took off up the stairs to the Attic. Eloise ran after him screeching You Basketcase! I'll Eviscerate you when I catch up wit' ya! But Oskar was able to leap out the window to relative safety, leaving Eloise to sigh plaintively, Aw, it's such a Garish Monde we live in.

unexpected

UNEXPECTED

combinations

COMBINATIONS

of design

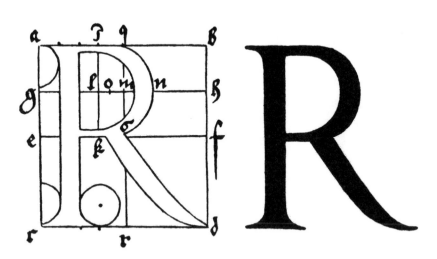

◀ Experimental type designs: Grunge fonts, 1996, 27.4 × 14.7 cm.
From: Robin Williams and John Tollett, *A Blip in the Continuum: A Celebration of Grunge Typography!*, 1996, Peachpit Press.

▲ *Bosozoku*, 2015.

▲ Constructed R by Albrecht Dürer, 1525.
From: Albrecht Dürer, *Of the Just Shaping of Letters*, 1965, Dover Publications.

Which one is ideal?

Which one is ideal?

Which one is ideal?

Which one is ideal?

Which one is ideal?

While no longer in

made from plastic

coffee cup stirrers

⬥ Versions of *Garamond*: American Type Founders, 1918; Monotype, 1923; Stempel, 1926; International Typeface Corporation, 1975; Adobe, 1989, 2005.

▲ *White no sugar*, 1997, Fuse.

▶ Some classic script typefaces: *Gong*, 1953, Wagner; *Mistral*, 1953, Olive; *Ashley Script*, 1955, Monotype; *Choc*, 1955, Olive
From: William Turner Berry, A.F. Johnson, W.P. Jaspert, *The Encyclopedia of Type Faces*, 1962, Blandford Press.

A B C D E F G H I J K L M N O P Q R S T
U V W X Y Z Blümen 1234567890
abcddeenafffflflghchijkcklllmnopqrsst
tßzüvwxyzg

ABCDEFGHIJKLMNOPQRSTUVWXYZ
abcdefghijklmnopqrstuvwxyz
1234567890
Strong, cold, northwesterly wind.
Lasts only one or two days.
Common in winter and spring.

ABCDEFGHIJKLMNOPQRST
UVWXYZ 12345
abcdefghijklmnopqrstuvwxyz

ABCDEFGHIJKLMNOPQRSTUVWXY
abcdefghijklmnopqrstuvwxyzabcdefghijkl
1234567890

egg gag gig igg badge cadge caged fadge gauzily

It is vital to know whether your guppy does indeed lay eggs or not, so that you will know what to expect in your tank. You also need to know so that you will be ready for when your guppy is about to give birth. Not only guppies, but there are also other fish in the ocean who in fact are not capable of laying eggs. They precisely are able to give birth specifically to 'live' fish.

It is vital to know whether your guppy does indeed lay eggs or not, so that you will know what to expect in your tank. You also need to know so that you will be ready for when your guppy is about to give birth. Not only guppies, but there are also other fish in the ocean who in fact are not capable of laying eggs.

Because External Situation Music Obviously Queen

⬆ *Akzidenz Grotesk*, 1898, Berthold, with the typical grotesque **g**.

▲ *Futura*, 1927, Bauer.

⬆ Left: *Akzidenz Grotesk*, right: *Futura*

6 Convention

Reading functions due to convention: the knowledge shared by readers of a particular script, the generally accepted forms of letters and other typographic signs. This know-how, embedded in the brain, makes reading into a custom – close to an automatism[a] – and ensures that readers have no difficulties in processing letters and lines of a text while concentrating on its content. Typefaces that are considered to be conventional may differ in basic shapes and details, but they can all be read effortlessly. This makes convention a powerful and challenging ingredient in type design: you can accept it or rebel against it but it is impossible to ignore. Type designers who are aware of typographic convention can negotiate it, and choose to stay close to the centre or to go near the edge. A generous amount of conventionality in a type design allows for quick and easy decoding of typeset language [see chapter 21]. How does this work?

For the recognition of letterforms two models have been proposed: template matching and feature detection. For template matching we should have stored in our brains complete representations of every variation of all typographic signs, and an incoming signal would be compared with all the templates, which makes this model unwieldy. Feature detection seems to be more efficient, involving the recognition of signs by detecting salient details and making quick comparisons. This is the model preferred by researchers, and it suggests that parts of letters are what matters during reading.[1] What do these parts look like? Where and how are they processed in our brains?

Inside everyone's head, behind the left ear is located 'the brain's letterbox', one of the many parts of the brain that enable us to read.[b] The letterbox extracts 'invariant representations' of letters and ignores all kinds of specifics such as type size, weight, thick and thin parts, roman or italic, probably also capitals and lowercase and all details. 'The … area seems to be a mosaic of … element detectors'.[2] So it seems that recognition of letters and other typographic signs is based on abstractions of letterforms and not on complete and very detailed signs. The multiplicity of

a] A dictionary definition of 'automatism' is: 'involuntary functioning'. Reading is partly controlled action as attention is directed intentionally on a text. From there on reading is a reflexive or responsive action, nearly automatic. — http://www.thefreedictionary.com/automatism (18/05/2017).

b] Dehaene (2003), pp 30–33; Dehaene (2009), pp 20, 21, 63. In his article from 2003 Dehaene called this part of the brain 'the visual word form area', a misnomer, as we do not initially recognize words but instead their component letters, enabling the brain to identify words almost instantaneously; see Larson (2004), pp 74–77. In his book from 2009, Dehaene calls the same cerebral area 'the brain's letterbox' and he states 'that global word shape does not play any role in reading.' (pp 20, 21).

letterforms many readers encounter daily is reduced to essentials detected and recognized by the brain's letterbox.

The many characteristics of typefaces, all the details stripped away by the letterbox, are recognized as well, otherwise typographic variations such as bold and italic would have no meaning for readers, and a typeface with special characteristics to express an identity, for instance, would make no sense. However, readers do discern and process the minutiae of letterforms, probably while the letterbox does its job – much parallel processing goes on during reading.[3] Meanwhile whole letters are perceived, just as we discern faces, cars, and all other objects in their entirety. Anything we look at is disassembled by the brain, processed in parts, and put back together again instantly and perceived as a whole.[4] It is possible that we recognize entire letters as well as all possible variations of letters with 'abstract letter detectors', 'neurons that can distinguish the identity of a letter in its various guises'.[5]

Where does conventionality end? A type design will certainly be seen as unconventional when the letterforms are difficult to recognize, as in the *New Alphabet* (1967) by Wim Crouwel (1928–). Between this design and the letters made by Garamond is a sliding scale without a clear point where conventionality ends and unconventionality begins. A typeface that may be perceived by users as having somewhat unconventional details can become accepted in a few years, with its unconventional aspects overlooked. In this way it moves closer to the centre of the type cloud; a type design can become acceptable to a large readership with very conventional basic shapes but unusual details. My *Swift* (1985) is a case in point, with its unusually large serifs and flat horizontal parts of curves – high-shouldered at the top of the x-height and attached very low to verticals just above the baseline – and on the whole rather angular. For a few years after publication these characteristics drew much comment and made some typographers decide not to use *Swift*. However, this criticism dissolved within a few years and *Swift* became widely used.

1. Rayner, Pollatsek (1989), pp 11–15.
2. Dehaene (2003), p 3; Dehaene (2009), pp 21, 22.
3. Dehaene (2009), pp 11, 43, 46, 47; Rayner, Pollatsek (1989), pp 14, 62, 80–83; Smith (1994), pp 241, 266.
4. Unger (2007), p 75.
5. Dehaene (2009), p 20.

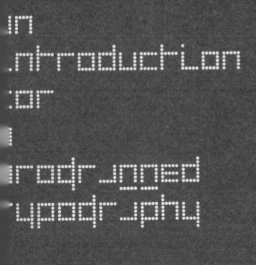

neu
alphabet

bbibility	een	une	eine
r	nodelijkheid	pobbibilite	noqlichtelt
	door	pour	fur
	de	le	die
velopnent	nieuwe	developnent	neue
	ontwikkeling	nouveju	entwicklung

in
introduction
for
i
rodrummed
typodraphy

▲ Wim Crouwel, 1967, *New Alphabet*,
250 × 250 mm, De Jong & Co.

The Emperors' Superfood

The hardened saliva nests of the edible-nest swiftlet and the black-nest swiftlet have been used in Chinese cooking for over 400 years, most often as bird's nest soup.

Over-harvesting of this expensive delicacy has led to a decline in the numbers of these swiftlets, especially as the nests are also thought to have health benefits and aphrodisiac properties. Most nests are built during the breeding season by the male swiftlet over a period of 35 days. They take the shape of a shallow cup stuck to the cave wall. The nests are composed of interwoven strands of salivary cement and contain high levels of calcium, iron, potassium, and magnesium.

▲ *Swift*, 1985, Hell.

7 Exemplary designs and themes

Type designers cannot base a design on the invariant representations of letters in the brain's letterbox – these are brief moments of cerebral activity during reading, flashes of recognition. We do not know what they look like.[a] Gill's norms and Morison's general idea represent convention, as does the stellar cloud of type designs. Convention is the result of the habituation required for easy reading and reciprocally influences the design of type. However, a type design cannot be based solely on convention, which serves instead as a flexible boundary you can respect, push, or climb over.

a] Brody (2012), pp 26, 46, 50, 62, 296, 306. It has been attempted to create type designs from parts of letters, but there is no certainty whether any of these comes close to the invariant representations; see Beier (2012), p 75. Sofie Beier shows 'the areas we use to identify letters'. These parts may be closer to what the brain's letterbox extracts, but, as they are based on *Arial*, they are not invariant.

Frutiger's essence of a letter is helpful as a visible phenomenon, but it was made after the fact; it shows how personality can play a role throughout a type designer's career, and as a basic shape it refers to convention as well. The typefaces of Garamond, which Tschichold was so enthusiastic about, give type designers something manifest: a specific example, not so much a single design as a body of designs from a particular period in history with distinct characteristics. It is a theme and as such provides designers with a concrete starting point.

Many type designs have long pedigrees. During the second half of the eighth century the Carolingian minuscule came to fruition; some six hundred years later, in the decades around 1400, it influenced the writing of humanist scholars, which in turn was the basis for typefaces used by Nicolas Jenson (around 1470) and Aldus Manutius (around 1495). Four hundred years on, Jenson's letterforms were revived, for example, as William Morris' *Golden Type* (1892), the typeface of the Doves Press (1900), as Monotype *Veronese* (1911, a distant relative of Jenson's type),[1] *Centaur* (1929) by Bruce Rogers (1870–1957), and *Adobe Jenson* (1996) by Robert Slimbach (1956–). Claude Garamond had as the model for his designs a copy of *De Aetna* by Pietro Bembo (1495), with a typeface cut by Francesco Griffo and printed by Aldus Manutius.[2] This type design was revived as *Bembo* (1929) by the English Monotype Corporation.[b]

b] *Bembo* is one of the great type designs of the twentieth century, not a literal revival but more a modern industrial design based on Griffo's typeface.

The first sanserif printing type (1816), a set of capitals published by William Caslon IV (1780–1869), goes straight back to a Roman republican inscription c] Mosley (1999), pp 38–40. John Lane (https://en.wikipedia.org/wiki/Caslon_ Egyptian) (06/05/2017), who has examined surviving Caslon specimens, suggests that the design is actually slightly earlier and may date to around 1812–14, noting that it appears in some undated but apparently earlier specimens. James Mosley mentions a date of 1816, 'or perhaps a bit earlier' (http:// typefoundry.blogspot.nl/2007/01/ nymph-and-grot-update.html) (06/05/2017).

from the early first century BC on the temple of Vesta in Tivoli.[c] These are ancient geometric capitals with perfectly circular **O**'s – a characteristic of *Futura* (1927), too. (As has been mentioned above in chapter 5, the capitals of *Futura* have a Roman background.) In 1988 Adrian Frutiger's *Avenir* fused three elements: geometric sanserif (*Futura*), Grotesque (such as *Helvetica*, 1957), and a more 'humanist' sanserif like *Gill Sans* (1928). (Frutiger's own, eponymous typeface of 1976 must also have had an influence.)[d] The capitals of *Avenir* come surprisingly close to the sanserif capitals of William Caslon IV;[3] and Frutiger's fusion became a theme for the following decades.

d] Osterer (2008), p 332. 'Grotesque' refers to those sanserifs developed late in the nineteenth century on the basis of the modern-face structure, also called the Didot-Bodoni model. *Helvetica* is labeled as a neo-grotesque. Sanserifs like *Gill Sans* are often called 'humanist' as their structure is derived from humanistic handwriting, basically the ancestor of all old-face type designs.

Such themes have often played a role in type design and are taken up again and again by new generations of designers for new readers. They are adapted to changes in time, tastes, and technology, and to new functions, to new genres of text. In these processes Gill's type-bodies change unnoticeably, while their clothes change visibly.

One of the major themes of the twentieth-century was typeface revival, which emerged as the history of type design was written. For instance, letterforms made by Robert Granjon (*c.* 1513–1589) came back as *Plantin* in 1913, *Galliard* in 1978 by Matthew Carter (1937–), and *Lyon* in 2006 by Kai Bernau (1978–). A type by Christoffel van Dijck (1606/7–69) was the example for *Van Dijck* (1935), and *Fournier* (1925) reflects the work of Pierre-Simon Fournier le jeune (1712–1768). The typeface of John Baskerville (1706–1775) has been revived and revised often, notably in 1996 as *Mrs Eaves*, named after Baskerville's wife, by Zuzana Licko (1961–). William Caslon I (1692–1766) admired and followed the letterforms of Christoffel van Dijck;[4] William Addison Dwiggins (1880–1956) took Scotch (1837)[5] as the starting point for the design of *Caledonia* (1938);[6] Fred Smeijers (1961–) based *Renard* (1992) on letterforms cut by Hendrik van den Keere (*c.*1541–1580).[7] The list is much longer.

Sanserif is another modern theme: it became prominent in the 1920s, especially in 1928 when Jan Tschichold proclaimed that this could be the only contemporary kind of typeface, simple and unadorned;[8] serifs were thought to be ornaments and had to go, while capitals were also deemed unnecessary by some modernists. In the meantime the theme of the modern sanserif was being developed in two directions, with the appearance of *Futura* in 1927 in Germany, and *Gill Sans* in 1928 in Great Britain. Both were overtaken in the 1950s with the publication of sanserifs such as *Univers* (1957), designed by Adrian Frutiger, and *Helvetica* (1957) designed by Max Miedinger (1910–1980), supported by a renewed Modern Movement with a very systematic approach to typography, using grids. *Gill Sans* disappeared from view for a while to return as a source of inspiration for later humanist sanserifs. An example of this category is *Syntax* (1968), designed by Hans Eduard Meier (1922–2014), related to seriffed old-face designs, while *Univers* and *Helvetica* have a modern-face structure [see chapters 4 and 7].

A theme related to sanserif originated with the so-called Egyptian typefaces, the first of which was shown in 1815 in a type specimen of Vincent Figgins (1766–1844).[9] Around 1845 these chunky letterforms, with heavy slab serifs, evolved into the more elegant Clarendons and Ionics,[10] which in turn led to a famous series of newspaper typefaces, the 'Linotype legibility group', starting with *Ionic* (1925).[11] This face and its successors were popular in the newspaper industry till deep into the twentieth century. Shortly after the publication of *Futura*, Egyptians went geometric, too, with the publication of, for example, *Memphis* (1929), *Beton* (c. 1931–1936), and *Rockwell* (1933).

Old face and modern face are two very broad themes. Old face covers a long period with type designs from shortly after the invention of printing up to those of William Caslon I and Pierre-Simon Fournier le jeune from the first half of the eighteenth century. Modern faces were first made by François-Ambroise Didot (1732–1793) cooperating with the punchcutter Pierre-Louis Vafflard (dates unknown) in 1784.[12] The period in between is called 'transitional', with, for instance, the *Romain du Roi* (1696–1702) for the French king Louis XIV and the letterforms of John Baskerville. So the old face and the transitional periods overlap, while the change from transitional to modern face took place in almost a single decade.[13] The category of old face encompasses what in classifications are called Renaissance letterforms (including *Garamond*) and those of the Baroque period (such as types by Christoffel van Dijck and Nicholas Kis (1650–1702), while the designs made from around 1784 are labelled Classicist or Neoclassical (Didot and Bodoni primarily). These three time periods are themes in themselves.

Many designs have not been based on historical examples, such as *Electra* (1935) by William A. Dwiggins, which is an original design. *Electra*'s basic shapes are conventional, but many of its details are not. The serifs at the baseline are rectangular and smallish, horizontal and slightly bracketed, while the serifs at the top of the x-height are heavier and slightly sloping, and at the top of the ascenders they are thinner again and also slightly inclined. Curves like the one of the **d** are generously round and touch the stems at very wide angles, while such very round curves are combined with angular parts, as in the top right part of the **a** and **n**.

In a specimen for *Electra* Dwiggins has a discussion with Kobodaishi, the (fictional) patron saint of lettering from Japan, and asks him what contemporary letterforms should look like, saying at one point: 'People are used to type that looks like ... [those made in Venice before 1500].' Kobodaishi protests: 'People are used to newspaper types, and typewriter types.' And he suggests thinking of: 'Electricity, ... sparks, energy – high speed steel – metal shavings coming off a lathe ....' And Dwiggins concludes: '... I can't quite see the metal shavings part, ... the flat way the curves get away from the ... stems: that is a speed product.'[14] The angularity of *Electra* and its emphasized horizontality are reminiscent of the handling of forms in the Art Deco style (1920s and 1930s), which was an influence on architecture, the design of furniture, jewellery, cars, and other everyday objects such as radios – and also on typefaces.

Many more original type designs have been made, such as *Antique Olive* (1962–1966) by Roger Excoffon (1910–1983), which is a trifle top-heavy due to the highest horizontal parts being slightly heavier than the other horizontals. Type designs with a much more outspoken reversed contrast appeared in the nineteenth century, for example in America with names like *French Clarendon* or *French Antique*.[15] In Britain such letterforms were called Italian (in France Italiennes).[16] *Antique Olive* is a much more subtle design and a personal response of Excoffon to popular sanserifs such as *Helvetica* and *Univers* (both 1957). In 1992 *Balance* by Evert Bloemsma (1958–2005) was published, clearly inspired by *Antique Olive*. And recently the reversed-contrast theme was taken up again, for example by Elena Papassissa (1983–) with *Dr Jekyll & Miss Hyde* (2012).

One more theme: hybrids – typefaces in which different ideas or themes are mixed. In the chapter on italics a mix of upright italic and roman letterforms will be mentioned, which has now become an accepted member of the type family known as 'informal' [see chapter 16]. A very different kind of hybrid is the merging of Fraktur, roman (Antiqua in German), and elements of Jugendstil early in twentieth-century Germany, such as *Behrens-Schrift* (1902) designed by architect Peter Behrens (1868–1940) and executed by the Rudhardische Giesserei, later (from 1906) the Klingspor Foundry.[17] Recently this theme has returned, without the Jugendstil motif, with various semi-Gothic type designs like *Fakir* (2010) by Underware,[e] *Eskapade* (2012) by Alisa Nowak (1983–) and *Paroli* (2014) by Elena Schneider (1981–).

e] Underware, based in The Hague, the Netherlands, was founded in 1999 by Bas Jacobs, Sami Kortemaki and Akiem Helmling.

1. *Veronese* was cut especially for J.M. Dent's Everyman's Library.
2. Barker (1974), p 11.
3. Osterer (2008), p 335.
4. Reed (1952), p 42.
5. De Vinne (1900), pp 212, 248.
6. Dwiggins (1939), pp vij–xij.
7. Smeijers (1996), pp 184, 185.

8. Tschichold (1928), p 75.
9. Gray (1976), pp 25, 26. Early sanserifs were also called Egyptians, see Gray (1976), p 38.
10. Gray (1976), p 66.
11. Hutt (1967), pp 55, 57, 58.
12. Unger (2001), pp 165–191.
13. Unger (2001), pp 165–191.
14. Dwiggins (1935), pp 34–38.
15. Kelly (1977), pp 129–135.
16. Gray (1976), p 34; Thibaudeau (1921), pp 432–434.
17. Burke (1992), pp 19–37; Burke (1998b), pp 32–39.

CHAPTER IV. NOW HALLBLITHE TAKETH THE SEA.

OW must it be told of Hallblithe that he rode fiercely down to the sea shore, and from the top of the beach he gazed a, bout him, and there be, low him was the Ship, stead and rollers of his kindred, whereon lay the three longships, the Sea, mew, and the Osprey and the Erne. Heavy and huge they seemed to him as they lay there, black,sided, icy,cold with the washing of the March waves, their golden dragon,heads look, ing seaward wistfully. But first had he looked out into the offing, and it was only when he had let his eyes come back from where the sea and sky met, and they had beheld nothing but the waste of waters, that he beheld the Ship,stead closely; and therewith he saw where a little to the west of it lay a skiff, which the low wave of the tide lifted and let fall from time to time. It had a mast, and a black sail hoisted thereon and flapping with slackened sheet. A man sat in the boat clad in black raiment, and the sun smote a gleam from the helm on his head. Then Hall, blithe leapt off his horse, and strode down the sands shouldering his spear; and when he came

12

centum quinque annis. et genuit enos · Uixit
que seth postquam genuit enos octingentis sep
tem annis. genuitque filios et filias · Et facti
sunt omnes dies seth nongentorum duodecim
annorum et mortuus e · Uixit uero enos no
naginta annis et genuit cainan · Post cuius
ortum . uixit octingentis quindecim annis .
et genuit filios et filias · Factaque sunt omnes
dies enos. nongentorum quinq: annorum . et

nica ad graecorum petition
mi regis tempore aedidit. C
caldeo sermone Dña pater
mus in graecum transtulit

◄ William Morris, *Golden Type*, as used in
his book *The Glittering Plain*, 1891,
The Kelmscott Press, 20.1 × 14.2 cm.
MUSEUM MEERMANNO, PHOTO RICKEY TAX

▲ Carolingian minuscule, 871–877. Enlarged.
From: The Second Bible of Charles the Bald.
BIBLIOTHÈQUE NATIONALE PARIS

▲ The humanistic handwriting of Felice
Feliciano, 1446 (probably 1466). Enlarged.
From: Eugenio di Palermo, *Erytraea Sybilla
Babylonica*, 1446.
BIBLIOTECA CIVICA VERONA

A distant relative
A distant relative

Generally, a relative who is a third cousin or greater, or a great-grand aunt/uncle. But the relative should only be considered 'distant' when you have little or no involvement with him or her.

Sometimes a third or a fourth cousin can be very close to you.

⬨ *Veronese*, 1911, Monotype.

▲ *Centaur*, 1929, Monotype.

▲ *Jenson*, 1996, Adobe.

▼ *Bembo*, 1929, Monotype.

The model for hi

W CASLON JUNR   LETTERFOUNDER

▲ The first sanserif type: William Caslon IV, Two lines English Egyptian, 1816. Reduced.
From: Nicolete Gray, *Nineteenth Century Ornamented Typefaces*, 1976, Faber and Faber.

▲ The inscription on the Temple of Vesta at Tivoli, early first century BC. Drawing, dated 1763, by George Dance. Reduced.
@ SIR JOHN SOANES MUSEUM, LONDON

▶ *Avenir*, 1988, Linotype.

Before the first stars
Before the first stars
Before the first stars
Before the first stars
Before the first stars
Before the first stars

The only three heavy elements in the universe that aren't made in stars. Despite originating from an incredibly hot, dense state, arbitrarily heavy elements weren't created early on the same way they're made today in stars. Despite being hot enough to make pretty much anything, the early universe makes almost nothing for one simple reason: if it was hot-and-dense enough to fuse elements together in the very early stages, it was also hot enough to blast those composite elements apart again.

lesigns.

hhhhhhhhhhhh
eeeeeeeeeeeee
lllllllllllllllllllllll
vvvvvvvvvvvvvv
eeeeeeeeeeeee
ttttttttttttttttttttttt
iiiiiiiiiiiiiiiiiiiiiii
ccccccccccccc
aaaaaaaaaaaaa

Superimposition of two-dimensional images containing correlated periodic grid structures may produce moiré patterns. Superimposition of two correlated layers comprising parallel lines or curves may give rise to line moiré patterns. The movement of one of the layers results in a faster movement of the line moiré superimposition image.

≜ *Helvetica*, 1957, Haas, Stempel.

▲ *Frutiger*, 1976, Linotype.

▶ Robert Granjon's *Gros Cicero*, here named 'Cicero Romain Gros Œil', c. 1560, from the specimen of Claude Lamesle, 1742, actual size.

SPECIAL COLLECTIONS, UNIVERSITY OF AMSTERDAM LIBRARY

CICERO ROMAIN GROS ŒIL,
Numero XXXIV.

Outre ces Divinitez communes & univerſelles, dont nous avons parlé juſqu'à préſent, il y en avoit d'autres dans la créance des Payens, qui n'étoient attachées qu'au bien particulier, ou des maiſons, ou des perſonnes.

Les Dieux domeſtiques s'appelloient Lares, ou bien, Penates, & étoient ſouvent de petits Marmouſets attachez en divers lieux de la maiſon, qu'ils honoroient comme leurs protecteurs, & de tems en tems leur offroient des ſacrifices de vin & d'encens.

Chacun encore, à leur dire, naiſſoit avec deux Génies, propres & particuliers, qu'on nommoit Démons, l'un deſquels étoit le bon, qui les portoit au bien, & leur procuroit toutes ſortes de proſperitez convenables à leur condition. L'autre au contraire leur étoit ennemi, & ne leur cauſoit que malheur, lorſqu'il devenoit le plus puiſſant.

Après tout cela ils reconnoiſſoient auſſi une Fortune, qui tenoit en ſa puiſſance les honneurs, les richeſſes, & les autres biens de cette vie, pour les donner, ou pour les ôter à qui bon lui ſembloit; mais qui étoit une Divinité aveugle & très-inconſtante, maniant une rouë qu'elle tournoit inceſſament, mettant la condition des uns & des autres, tantôt en haut & tantôt en bas, de ſorte qu'elle n'avoit rien de ferme ni d'aſſuré. Elle étoit adorée de la plûpart des hommes, & les grands Princes en conſervoient communément une hors de chez eux, pour leur être toujours favorable.

Je ne parle point ici, ni de la Déeſſe Nemeſis, qui avoit l'œil ſur les crimes d'un chacun, pour les venger, ni du Dieu Momus, qui ſe rendoit mépriſable & odieux à cauſe de ſes mauvaiſes qualitez. Car il ne tiroit ſa naiſſance que du ſommeil & de la nuit; & encore qu'il fût très-fainéant & inhabile à tout, c'étoit néanmoins un bavard, qui vouloit parler de tout, & trouvoit à redire ſur tous les autres; ce qui provenoit tant de ſa vanité, que de la foibleſſe de ſon eſprit: comme c'eſt l'ordinaire de ces eſprits critiques, qui contre-

Mon bonheur me parut d'abord établi d'une manière inébranlable, Manon était la douceur et la complaisance même; elle avait pour moi des attentions si délicates, que je me crus trop parfaitement dédommagé de toutes mes peines. Comme nous avions acquis tous deux un peu d'expérience, nous raisonnâmes sur la solidité de notre fortune. Soixante mille francs, qui faisaient le fond de nos

In the first place, novelty in very spectacular form had been woven profusely into the twentieth century texture. "We should be amazed indeed," wrote Carl Becker in 1932, "if tomorrow and tomorrow and tomorrow failed to offer us something new to challenge our capacity for readjustment."

créance des Payens, qui n'étoie
créance des Payens, qui n'étoie

⬟ *Plantin*, 1913, Monotype.

▲ *Galliard*, 1978, Linotype.

▲ Above: Robert Granjon's *Gros Cicero*, c. 1560. Below: *Galliard*, 1978, Linotype. Enlarged.
From: Preston Gralla, 'Man of Letters', 1989, in: PC *Computing*.

Nor had this novelty been confined to a steady stream of astonishing technological inventions. In politics and economics, in law and education, in family life and the composition of social classes, sweeping transformation have occured. The fine arts of our century have created a copious array of novel objects, and a great variety of novel schools. Our theoretical sciences have provide a prodigious bounty of new facts, and a great diversity of new theory.

▲ *Lyon*, 2006, Commercial Type.

Mogelijk kwam Christoffel van Dijck kort voor 1640 naar Amsterdam om als leerling-gezel bij een goudsmid te werken. Uit een akte opgemaakt voor zijn huwelijk op 11 september 1642 blijkt dat hij op dat moment 36 jaar was, en voordien nooit gehuwd was geweest. Hij trouwde met Swaentje Harmens, de weduwe van Joh. de Praet. Zijn adres is dan in de Breestraat, beroep: lettergieter. In een latere akte uit 1642 wordt hij aangeduid als goudsmid gevestigd in de Breestraat.

Fournier's contributions to printing were his creation of initials and ornaments, his design of letters, and his standardization of type sizes.

HEAVENLY CHOCOLATE

Indulge yourself with heavenly chocolate that tastes incredible but without the guilt. Decadently creamy but without all the unhealthy ingredients.

We are asked hundreds of times per month for free samples. Unfortunately, as we are not a massive corporate company, we cannot say yes to everyone who asks.

◈ *Van Dijck*, 1935, Monotype.   ▲ *Mrs Eaves*, 1996, Emigre.

▲ *Fournier*, 1925, Monotype.

Nowadays most researchers agree that it does not exist a one-size-fit-all design process and this situation has been reported in a lot of application contexts.

Besides organizations are often composed of a limited number of people, with specific skills and competencies; hence, these organizations cannot use all kinds of design processes without spending too much time in personnel formation; all of that let the cost of producing a system increasing more and more.

▲ *Caledonia*, 1938, Linotype.

▲ *Renard*, 1992, The Enschedé Font Foundry.

Different well known approaches present different definitions

definitions

definitions

definitions

definitions

definitions

definitions

In order to create the new design process, the method designer needs to have access to a repository of components.

▲ *Univers*, 1957, Deberny & Peignot.

▲ *Syntax*, 1968, Stempel.

From an advertisement in "The Athenian Ga-zette" of 1696, it appears that the Coffee-houses

ABCDEFGHIJKLMNOPQRSTUVWXYZÆŒ £ 1234567890 &

In the State Lotteries, now wisely abolished by the Legislature, the risk

A B C D E F G H I J K L M N O P Q R
S T U V W X Y Z & Æ Œ
abcdefghijklmnopqrstuvwxyz
fi fl ff ffi ffl æ œ 1 2 3 4 5 6 7 8 9 0
A B C D E F G H I J K L M N O P Q R S T U V
W X Y Z & Æ Œ

▲ Vincent Figgins, an early Egyptian: *Double Pica Antique*, 1828. Reduced.
From: Nicolete Gray, *Nineteenth Century Ornamented Typefaces*, 1976, Faber and Faber.

▲ Caslon, *Double Pica Ionic*, 1844. Reduced.
From: Nicolete Gray, *Nineteenth Century Ornamented Typefaces*, 1976, Faber and Faber.

▲ *Ionic*, 1925, Linotype.

▶ *Memphis*, 1929, Stempel.

Egyptian geometry refers to geometry as it was developed and used in Ancient Egypt. Ancient Egyptian mathematics as discussed here spans a time period ranging from c. 3000 BC to c. 300 BC.

We only have a limited number of problems from ancient Egypt that concern geometry. Geometric problems appear in both the Moscow Mathematical Papyrus (MMP) and in the Rhind Mathematical Papyrus (RMP). The examples demonstrate that the Ancient Egyptians knew how to compute areas of several geometric shapes and the volumes of cylinders and pyramids. Also the Egyptians used many sacred geometric shapes such as squares and triangles on temples and obelisks.

Concrete
is a composite material
composed of fine and
coarse aggregate
bonded together with
a fluid cement that
hardens over time.

**Rocks are composed
of grains of minerals,
which are
homogeneous solids
formed from a
chemical compound
arranged in an orderly
manner.**

▲ *Beton*, c. 1931–1936, Bauer.　　　　▲ *Rockwell*, 1934, Monotype.

puritas ad curam apostolicæ sedis potissimum per-
tinere cognoscitur, ideo Pius IV pontifex maximus,
pro sua in omnes Ecclesiæ partes incredibili vigi-
lantia, lectissimis aliquot sanctæ romanæ Ecclesiæ cardinalibus, aliisque tum sacrarum litterarum
tum variarum linguarum peritissimis viris, eam
provinciam demandavit ut vulgatam editionem
latinam, adhibitis antiquissimis codicibus manu-

Mon nom par la victoire est si bien affermi,
Qu'on me croit dans la paix un lion endormi :
Mon réveil incertain, du monde fait l'étude,
Mon repos en tous lieux jette l'inquiétude,
Et tandis qu'en ma Cour les aimables loisirs,
Ménagent l'heureux choix des jeux & des plaisirs,
Pour envoyer l'effroi sous l'un & l'autre pole,
Je n'ai qu'à faire un pas & hausser la parole.

CORNEILLE.

Afcendonica Romeyn.
Quod quifque in ano eft, fci
unt. Sciunt Id qui in Aurum
Rex reginæ dixerit : Sciunt
quod Juno; Neque & futura
in Æ ABCDEFGHIKLMN
OPRSTVWXU Y Σ ffl ffl *
([§ † ? ✠ e‿ ABCDEFGHIKLMNO

▲ François-Ambroise Didot
and Pierre-Louis Vafflard, 1785,
the first truly modern face.
Enlarged.
From the 12mo bible printed 'Pour
l'Éducation de Monseigneur le
Dauphin'.

▲ Romain du Roi, 1696–1702.
From: Le Romain du Roi, 2002, Musée
de l'imprimerie, Lyon.

◀ Christoffel van Dijck,
Ascendonica Romeyn,
as shown in the specimen
of the widow of Daniel
Elsevier, 1681. Actual size.
From: Joseph Moxon, Mechanick
Exercises, 1978, Dover Publications.

Clein Canon Romein

Dominus ille omnium liberrimus, fumme bonus fumme potens fumme fapiens,in quem nulla cadit mutatio aut conversionis obumbratio, a quo per quem in quem omnia,in quo nos etiam vivimus movemur & fu

"But why *like* them?" he said. "You don't live in Venice in 1500. This is 1935. Why don't you do what *they* did: take letter shapes and see if you can't work them into something that stands for 1935? Why doll yourself up in Venetian fancy-dress costume and go dodging around in airplanes and automobiles dressed up *that* way?"

"I know" I said. "But you can't play tricks with the shapes of letters. If you do, people can't read 'em. People are used to type that looks like that, and you have got to keep mighty close to the old designs."

"Used to the 1500 types? Don't you believe it. People are used to newspaper types, and typewriter types. Your Venice types are just about as queer-look-

▲ Nicholas Kis, *Clein Canon Romein*,
as shown in the 'Amsterdam' specimen,
c. 1686. Actual size.
From: György Haiman, *Nicholas Kis*, 1983, Jack W.
Stauffacher / The Greenwood Press.

▲ *Electra*, 1935, Linotype. Actual size.

Trifles offer a rare combination of sensual and intellectual pleasures. How many times have I dipped my spoon into one and experienced in a succession the light frothy cream, the smooth velvety custard, the tangy fruit mingling with the bouquet of wine (or sherry or liqueur), and perhaps a touch of almondy crunchiness from ratafias of macaroons, and lastly the sweet, soft but crumbly texture of the sponge fingers.

▲ *Antique Olive*, 1962–1966, Olive.

◀ *French Antique*, c. 1869. Reduced. From: Rob Roy Kelly, *American Wood Type: 1828–1900*, 1977, Da Capo Press.

▼ *Balance*, 1992, FontFont.

▼ *Dr Jekyll & Miss Hyde*, 2012.

to remain upright and steady

Gabriel John Utterson
Richard Enfield

RTISTIC CONSIDERATIONS ⬦ The art of making a book an objekt of beauty has never stood higher than it did in Germany at the time when the art of printing was first invented. None of the successors of Gutenberg and his associates either at home or abroad have ever surpassed in strength or harmony the work, which they ex= ecuted, closely following the traditions of the old Gothic manuscripts. The German book had reached a second era of perfection at the time of the early renaissance when masters like Dürer, Cranach and Holbein made an artistic use of the wood cut, which had been invented and perfected in Germany, for the pictures and orna= mentation of books. Their example was followed until the Thirty Years War broke this flower like it did so many others. In the books of the 18th century the German copper=plate engraver rarely equalled his French prototype. The German book art be= gan to revive in the first decades of the 19th century, and styles in architec= ture and all dekorative arts, and follo= wed each other in quick succession. These changes of style are still par= tially reflected in the German book

▲ *Behrens-Schrift*, 1902, Rudhardsche Giesserei (Klingspor). Reduced.
From: Gustav Kühl, *On the Psychology of Writing*, 1905, Rudhardsche Giesserei.

In this otherworldly space of time, the surprise could be complete.

I have seen about as many *monkeyshines* from you as I will tolerate.

The object of the Paroli betting system is to obtain three consecutive wins in a row.

⬣ *Fakir*, 2010, Underware.　　　　　　▲ *Paroli*, 2014.

⬣ *Eskapade*, 2012, TypeTogether.

8 Technology, economy, pragmatism, and formalization

From the beginnings of typography, in the middle of the fifteenth century, technology has had much influence on letterforms, both in the making of typefaces as well as on their application in typography. Punchcutters, working with burins and files on a piece of steel, sculpting letterforms as small as 6 point (Didot, 2.26 mm), sometimes with an x-height of around 1 mm, were practically unable to make similar details exactly the same, despite their often astonishing precision. This led to 'irregularities of punchcutting, once lost to industrialization'[1] [see chapter 15], though they were sometimes reproduced by industry: an example is Monotype's *Caslon Old Face* (1916) having different top serifs and other variations.[2]

Until well into the eighteenth century the surface of paper, seen from the perspective of a 12-point letter, looked much like a freshly ploughed field. This influenced the appearance of type, caused its shapes to be varied by ink spreading around the letters, together with sometimes uneven inking, differences in pressure on the press, and the wear of type as a consequence of the relatively soft type metal. Around 1757 John Baskerville was one of the first to use wove paper with a finer texture than laid paper, further smoothed by hot pressing to achieve a more precise impression of letterforms.[a]

The first mechanical printing press with automatic inking was constructed in 1811 by Frederick Koenig (1774–1833) in England.[b] With mechanization, the precision of printing steadily increased, but it took until the introduction of computer-to-plate technology (CTP)[c] in 1995 for letterforms to finally appear on paper

a] Wove paper is made with a mould in which the wires were woven together like the threads of cloth, as distinct from laid paper, where the wires are *laid* side by side. The papermaker James Whatman has been credited with the introduction of wove paper around 1757. Turner Berry (1966), p 169.

b] The Dutch printer Willem Jansz. Blaeu of Amsterdam is credited with improvements of the wooden printing press in 1638. In 1772 Wilhelm Haas of Basle constructed a handpress of which the most important parts were made of metal instead of wood. Turner Berry (1966), pp 23, 181.

c] The first CTP installation was sold by the Canadian firm Creo. Information supplied by Henk Gianotten (05/01/2017).

precisely as shaped by type designers. With this technology a page made up on screen is digitally transferred directly onto a printing plate, without any of the intermediate steps of earlier technologies. When creating a newspaper typeface in the 1980s, designers had to take into account the effects of photo-typesetting and several stages of reproduction by camera, which rounded off and filled up all sharp corners.[d] Of course, these effects mainly affected text in small sizes. Indeed, until well into the 1980s, newspapers were still printed with thin inks on rough and soft paper. The surface of paper for newspapers (and for all printed products) has since then been much improved. On screens it took until the early twenty-first century for resolutions to become high enough to replicate letterforms faithfully, for example with Retina displays from 2012.[3]

d] Text for newspapers was often projected onto photographic paper instead of transparent film, which made for a fuzzier image than on film. Text was then pasted up on a piece of cardboard the size of a newspaper page, photographed in its entirety and turned into a large negative. This was then exposed onto an offset plate, or on a photopolymer plate to be printed by letterpress. Unger (1979), pp 134–149.

Other steps towards current ways of designing, producing, and distributing type were: the development of the first digital typesetting machine, the Digiset (1965); Ikarus digital outlines (1975);[e] the Macintosh computer (1984); the Postscript page-description language (1984), which eased the production and use of digital typefaces; PageMaker (1985), the first desktop publishing program; the Fontographer type-design software (1986); and the TrueType font format in 1991. Another link in this chain was the Apple Laserwriter (1985), which can be seen as a small typesetting machine and printing press. More recent, important developments are: OpenType (1996), a combination of two font-formats, Postscript and TrueType; the Web Open Font Format (WOFF, 2009), which has become the font format supported by all browsers; and OpenType Variable Fonts (2016).

e] The Ikarus software was developed by Dr. Peter Karow of URW in Hamburg and made public at the 1975 ATypI-conference in Warsaw.

These developments have removed nearly all obstacles between the design of type and its final appearance in texts on paper and on screen – typefaces are largely designed on screen and are often read on screen. While paper reflects light, emitted light from screens can impede reading text in small sizes if the background is too bright and outshines the letters.[4] Resolutions can still be relatively low on older screens, but nothing compared to those of the 1970s: for instance, 9 dots wide and 14 dots high, into which all letterforms had to be squeezed; or the 300 dots per inch (without hinting) of laser printers in the mid-1980s. An important objective of type designers then was: how to defy technology.

An effect of mechanization, from the end of the nineteenth century, was a very practical approach to type design: typographic pragmatism. One of the consequences of faster presses was an alleviation of pressure, causing the thin parts of typical nineteenth-century letterforms to disappear. Theodore Low

De Vinne, printer and historian, had a very practical solution for this problem: the thickening of these parts. Simultaneously he increased the x-height, giving the design a slightly condensed appearance. The result was *Century Expanded* (1896) executed by Linn Boyd Benton (1844–1932), the inventor of the punchcutting machine (1885) and father of the type designer Morris Fuller Benton (1872–1948).[5] Finding such straightforward solutions for technical hurdles spawned, for example, a famous group of newspaper typefaces, used successfully for decades [see chapter 7].

This kind of pragmatic thinking also provided solutions in the 1970s and 1980s for the first generation of digital typesetting machines, and for the photographic processing of letterforms. In the Digiset, developed by the firm of Dr.-Ing. Rudolf Hell GmbH in Kiel, Germany, letters were generated by a cathode ray tube, at a fairly coarse resolution, and projected on to photographic paper. The difficulty of reproducing existing type designs, such as any version of *Garamond*, with this technology was an impetus for Wim Crouwel to design his *New Alphabet* (1967), using horizontal and vertical lines only. However, more conventional type designs were soon made for this technology, such as *Marconi* (1976) by Hermann Zapf (1918–2015), and my own *Demos* (1976).[6] In 1986 the cathode ray tube in the Digiset was replaced by a laser beam, allowing for much higher resolutions and a much more faithful reproduction of letterforms.[7]

Digital technology has improved enormously and the opportunities for the enhancement of type designs and typography have been expanded, not only qualitatively but also with larger character sets containing signs for many different languages, and with fundamental advancements for the setting of text in other scripts than the Latin. It is now possible to achieve much more refined and varied typography than ever before. Compared to previous technologies that prevented a precise reproduction of letterforms, technology today does not hamper designers and users anymore, but offers expanding opportunities for accurate control over letterforms.

In newspapers and publications such as cheap paperbacks, it is desirable to get as much text on a page while maintaining ease of reading. *Times New Roman* (1932) is a fairly condensed design and has a large x-height [see chapter 10], with short ascenders and descenders as a consequence. This allows *Times* to be used in relatively small sizes, resulting in a few more characters per line and more lines per column or per page than is possible with many other typefaces. This principle has been followed successfully with other type designs for newspapers.[f] On screen economy rarely counts, though it makes sense for small handheld devices, for instance mobile phones with screens of approximately the width of a newspaper column.

f] For example *Swift* (1985) and *Gulliver* (1993), designed by the author, were both based on this scheme. In addition *Swift* had to put up resistance against the previously described effects of photosetting.

A consequence of the invention of typefounding (punchcutting, matrix making, and type casting), and later of mechanization and digitization, is the formalization of letterforms. Formalization is the process of reaching a consistent form or shape for letters and accompanying signs. Paleographers will agree that the Carolingian minuscule is quite formal, although it shows the unavoidable variations inherent in handwriting. With the reproduction of handwriting – both gothic and humanistic – in metal with each letter cast in large numbers from one and the same matrix, variation decreased. However, as described above, irregularities did not disappear entirely nor quickly.

Now formalization is fully attainable, with designers able to control letterforms and their combinations better than ever, and in minute detail with digital design. Some see this as a loss and want to regain the variations or irregularities of pre-digital or even pre-industrial typography. There is no evidence that punchcutters saw a need for inconsistencies[8] but with digital design these can be added deliberately, such as in *Beowolf* (1990) created by Erik van Blokland (1967–) and Just van Rossum (1966–): 'we decided to create a typeface that would add liveliness to the page that has since long been lost using the most modern technologies'.[9] [See also chapter 15] This sense of loss can also be the reason for an interest in alternate letterforms, even in reviving those made for earlier typefaces, such as *Futura*.[9]

g] Burke (1998a), pp 87, 92, 93, 103. See also Barker (1974), p 11, for alternates cut by Francesco Griffo for the typeface used in Pietro Bembo's *De Aetna*.

1. Tankard (2005), p 8.
2. Southall (2005), pp 42, 43.
3. https://en.wikipedia.org/wiki/Retina_Display, (05/02/2017).
4. http://journals.plos.org/plosone/article?id=10.1371/journal.pone.0083676 (22/06/2017).
5. Rollins (1968), pp 67–70.
6. Middendorp (2004), pp 166–174.
7. Kredel (1988), p 214.
8. Tankard (2008), pp 48, 49.
9. Van Blokland (1991), pp 27–29.

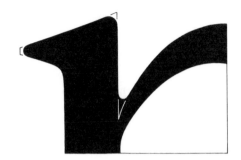

abcdefghijkl

▰ Left, the top of a 6-point (Didot) punch from the *Coronelle Romaine* cut by Hendrik van den Keere. *c.* 1570–1573, x-height: *c.* 1.1 mm. Right: the bottom of a matrix made with this punch. Enlarged.
MUSEUM PLANTIN-MORETUS, PHOTOS: FRED SMEIJERS

◥ Effects of phototypesetting: rounded off and filled up sharp corners.
From: Gerard Unger, 'The Design of a Typeface', 1979, *Visible Language*.

▲ *Caslon Old Face*, 1916, Monotype, with varying top serifs. Enlarged.

◀ Gerard Unger, 1984, part of a type design on a grid of 9 × 14 dots for Philips low-resolution screens. Enlarged.

▶ Gerard Unger, 1986, *Amerigo*,
Bitstream. Right: the original
drawing. Left: reproduction in low
reslution (300 dpi), to which the
design has been adapted.

▼ *Century Expanded*, 1896, American
Type Founders. Actual size.
From: Theodore Low De Vinne, *Types of the
De Vinne Press*, 1907.

▼ *Marconi*, 1976, Hell. Actual size.
From: *Catalogue of Typefaces*, 1983, Dr.-Ing.
Rudulf Hell GmbH.

CENTURY EXPANDED

THIS face of type was first made
on 10-point body, for use on
THE CENTURY MAGAZINE,
and it has been used for many books
of The Century Co. The expansion
of the letter is upward, enabling one
to get much matter in small space.

18-point. A. T. F. Co.

4,5 mm 12 pt, Durchschuß 0,375 mm 1 pt

Der digitale Lichtsatz erschließt uns für
die typografische Gestaltung des Satzes
neue Dimensionen. Dies gilt aber auch
für die Schriften, die sich in ihrem Stil
mit jeder Zeit ändern. Nicht nur viele
Schriftschöpfer, sondern auch die Setz-
und Druckmaschinen beeinflussen das
Aussehen aller Schriften. So ist es auch
heute im Lichtsatz. Der Digiset setzt die

Being pragmatic means being rational.

Although they only had an exclusive usage right for one year, they stuck with the typeface for forty years. In 1972 Times New Roman was replaced by Times Europa, which was a redesign adapted to faster presses and paper of lower quality. *The Times* entered the computer age in 1986 with Times Roman. The computer drawn version of the original Times New Roman did not make a quality impression and was therefore replaced by Times Millennium in 1991, which was the first version that was redesigned on a computer.

a g m n ä &

▲ *Demos*, 1976, Hell.

▲ *Times New Roman*, 1932, Monotype.

▲ Alternate lowercase letters for *Futura*, 1927. From an undated specimen of the Bauersche Giesserei.

Beowolf Beowolf
Beowolf Beowolf

AAAA
AaBbCcDdEeFf
GgHhIi&JjKkLl
MmNnOoPpQq
RrSsTtUuVvWw
XxYyZz!@#$%

▲ *Beowolf*, 1990, FontFont.
Erik van Blokland, Just van Rossum

9 Strokes and parts

According to the calligrapher Ewan Clayton (1956–), letters are 'made up of a carefully coordinated and limited sequence of proportionally related strokes, which the pen itself ensures are all related to each other as a result of ... the re-petitive and systematic thinking about the strokes that the [scribe] employs'.[a]

When you take up a writing instrument, dip it in ink, put these strokes together and leave the letters as they are, then the result can be called direct or organic. As soon as you start touching up the letters, for instance strengthening thin parts with a fine brush, regulariz-ing endings or correcting curves, then the letters become indirect or synthetic. Type designers go much further with planning, trying out, considering, detail-ing, and revising their work. All type designs are indirect or synthetic.

a] Clayton (2013), p 115. In this sen-tence Ewan Clayton mentions only the broad-nibbed pen. By omitting this ref-erence from the citation here, his text also applies to the pointed and flexible nib. See chapter 4, note 6.

The shapes of written strokes are made in a radically different way on screen: indirectly, by using control points with handles and segments of curves and straight lines between such points. Traces of the pen, often in a difference between thick and thin, or appearing as triangular serifs, are very stubborn and seem reluctant to leave letters, although in type designs these traces have often been so modified that when followed with a pen they turn out to be very different – they have become synthetic. In digital type design, parts of letters, such as serifs, can be easily repeated, modified and adapted. And composite parts, for example a foot serif with part of a stem attached, or even half a let-terform, are used as well. Such elements are assembled into letters, are moved from one character to another, temporarily positioned, and adapted or rede-signed and fed back to previously designed letters.

The use of repeatable and composite elements is not new. The American designer William A. Dwiggins used stencils as a step in his design process after having made rough pencil sketches first. Some of these stencils or templates are composite parts.[1] Repeating components of letters such as counters is common in digital type design, and was practised much earlier by, among oth-ers, Hendrik van den Keere. In his *Small Pica Roman* from shortly before 1580 the interior spaces of the **b, d, p,** and **q** and their accented versions are all the same and made with a counterpunch as an identical and interchangeable part.[2] Such parts can also be called modules – type design is to a degree modular design.[3]

This applies to the parts of letters (and other signs) as well as the spaces within and around the characters.

As soon as letters were cut in metal they were indirect, synthetic, although some details, such as foot-serifs, still occasionally showed traces of the broad-nibbed pen. Otherwise the pen-strokes as mini-gestures were gradually absorbed in mini-sculptures, the punches, used to strike matrices from which to cast type. The punches were made with burins and files from steel rods: material was taken away until letters remained, and in this process the penstrokes, the characteristics of written letters, were subtly transformed into the characteristics of printing types. For example, transitions from thick to thin or the shapes of serifs can be endlessly remodelled, sharpened or thickened, and regularized – which is what happened throughout the history of type design.

The strokes from which letters were originally built are small gestures, made by the hand and arm holding the pen. The muscle movements have an influence on the letterforms, which also can happen when outlines of letters are drawn by hand, giving tension to curves. Such a reflection of muscularity can also be achieved with the help of templates, French curves, or in other ways – with digital design too – if the designer is aware of this effect. Gudrun Zapf-von Hesse (1918–), for example, who is both a calligrapher and a type designer, fixed calligraphic movements in her type design *Diotima* (1951–1953).

The industrial manufacture of metal type, which lasted almost a hundred years from the end of the nineteenth century, proceeded as follows: sketches or precise drawings by a designer or an artist were adapted into large scale production drawings of outlines,[b] and then into patterns for making punches or matrices mechanically with the assistance of a pantograph.[c] Large production drawings were rarely made by designers themselves (Dwiggins did it[4]) but mostly by workers in a type drawing office, often women.[5] They were experts at handling pencils, rulers and French curves, interpreting original drawings while sticking to the requirements of mechanical typesetting. For parts that could be repeated, such as serifs, templates were sometimes used. This way of cooperating between designers and manufacturers continued until well into the 1980s.[d]

As a result of desktop computing, a lone type designer can create typefaces and carry out the production, marketing, and distribution, although cooperation with colleagues is often preferred. Digital technology has also opened up a large market for typefaces, with an increase in the number of type designers and independent

b] The first large-scale models we know about are those for the *Romain du Roi*, of which the first were made in 1695 as engravings. As the different type sizes were still cut by hand, the final letterforms show considerable differences with the engraved models. Dreyfus (1982), p 16.

c] Cost (2011), pp 130–138. At American Type Founders Linn Boyd Benton had developed an intricate system to scale type with the pantograph, to make all kinds of adjustments for small and large sizes.

d] In my practice it lasted until 1989, when I bought my first digital type-design equipment. Up to then I made large pencil drawings that were digitized with the Ikarus system by Elke Fahrenkrug, employee of Dr.-Ing. Rudolf Hell GmbH.

distributors, as well as a rise in the number of type designs. Type changed from tangible objects into immaterial images, and the time to create and produce a type design has shrunk drastically. And, as already mentioned, the design of type and its appearance in texts are now brought together in the same medium: typefaces are largely designed on screen and are often read from screen. Up to around 2014 type designs were primarily made to be printed on paper; now the main requirement is to appear on screens.[e]

In relation to the grammar of legibility [see chapter 3], type design involves creating all the signs necessary for the composition of legible language on screen, paper, or any other surface, such as walls or windows. All the strokes and parts, and all the signs built from these, function together as an entity; it has been said that the aim of the type designer is 'to create a beautiful group of letters and not a group of beautiful letters'.[f] The objective is well choreographed group behaviour and, to be sure of teamwork between all parts of letters and all other typographic signs, several fundamental attributes have to do their work: structure, pattern and texture, consistency and coherence, rhythm and space.

e] In 2007 or early 2008, for the first time in history, more people were living in cities than in the countryside. And it is likely that in 2013 or 2014 more people were reading from screens than from paper. This is difficult to ascertain with the information available on the web. – https://www.theguardian.com/environment/2007/jan/17/society.pollution (14/03/2017).

f] This statement has been attributed to Matthew Carter. Its origin is not known but Matthew thinks that Mike Parker first used it (e-mail exchange, 23/12/2016).

Carried by a framework of horizontal and vertical proportions, the main segments of letters – straight vertical parts as in the **n**, large curves and diagonals as in **O**, **o**, **V** and **v** – start the performance, soon joined by ascenders and descenders, horizontal straight parts, smaller curves and diagonals, as in the **a** and **k**, a part like the flag of the **r**, and many smaller details; then come the capitals, numerals, punctuation marks, and many other elements from the grammar of legibility. Serifs will be brought into play or omitted, or seriffed and sanserif letters cooperate. Letterforms with a high or moderate contrast can be considered, from very thin to ultra bold. And the balancing of interior and inter-character spaces is an important part of the choreography. With all these elements and considerations, many different typefaces can be designed – the number of variations is infinite.

1. Abbe (1979), pp 58, 59.
2. Smeijers (1996), p 113. See also Vervliet (1968), pp 274, 275.
3. Mooney (2014), *passim*. http://typeculture.com/academic-resource/articles-essays/modularity-an- elemental-approach-to-type-design/ (23/03/2017).
4. Dwiggins (1940), p 11.
5. Slinn (2014), p 190.

ˏ ˏ ɩ a ˊ a, ˋ l l ɔ b ˏ c c ˘ c ˏ c
c l d ˏ c ˆ c ‑ e ˏ ſ ſ ˆ ſ ˘ f ˏ c
ɔ o ˘ o ˏ g ɕ g ˏ ˊ l l ɿ h h ˏ ˊ ɩ
i ˏ ˊ ɩ l ɿ ñ ˏ ˢ l l ˏ ʞ ˏ ˂ k ˏ ˊ ɩ
l ˏ ˊ ɩ l ɿ n ɿ m m ˏ ˊ ɩ l ɿ n n
ɕ ɔ o ˏ ˊ l l ɔ p ɕ c l q q ˏ ˊ ɩ l
ˏ r ſ l ˆ ſ ˏ ˏ ˏ s s s ˏ l ˆ t ˏ ˊ
ɩ ɪ u ˏ ˉ ˎ ˎ ˎ x x ˏ ˉ ˎ / y ˏ
ˊ ˉ / 7 ˍ z ˏ

/ / ˎ ˄ ˄ ‑ A ˏ ˉ I I ˀ P ɔ Ɜ B ˏ ɕ C
C ˏ ˉ I I ɔ D ˏ ˉ I L L ˪ ˂ E ˏ ˉ I ſ ˂ F ˏ
ɕ C ˅ G G ˏ ˉ I I ſ II II ‑ H ˏ ˉ I I ˏ ˉ I
I ˊ ʞ ˎ ˂ K ˏ ˉ I L L ˏ ˉ I I ˎ ˎ / N ˎ
M M ˏ ˉ I I ſ ˉ II ˎ N ˏ ɕ ɔ O ˏ ˉ I I ˀ
P ˏ ɕ ɔ O ˍ Q ˏ I I ˀ P ɕ Ɂ R ˏ ˏ
ˏ ˏ ˏ s ˏ ˊ ˉ ˉ I T T ˏ ˉ ˎ / ˎ ˎ V ˏ
ˉ ˎ ˎ / ˎ x x ˏ ˉ ˎ ˏ ˎ ˏ I Y Y ˏ ˊ ˉ
/ 7 ˍ z z ˏ

o mnhrf

o tug

o cdeq

o as

o pb

◀ Letters and their parts based on pen
strokes.
From: Wolfgang Fugger, *Handwriting Manual*, 1960
(originally 1553), Oxford University Press.

▲ 'limited sequence of … related strokes,
which the pen ensures are all related'.
From: Gerrit Noordzij, *Gewone letters, Gerrit's early
models*, 2013, Geen bitter / De Buitenkant.

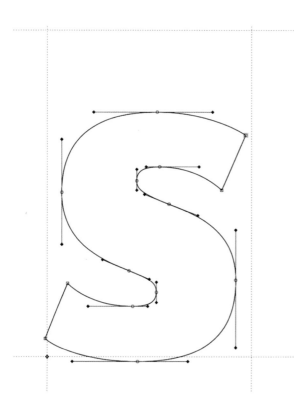

◀ Control points with handles on the contour of *Sanserata* black italic **s**, Gerard Unger, 2016, TypeTogether. (Screenshot)

▼ Parts, such as serifs, are moved from one character to another, temporarily positioned and adapted or redesigned and fed back to previously designed letters. Sergio Trujillo, *Satira* black, 2015. MA Typeface Design of the University of Reading. (Screenshot)

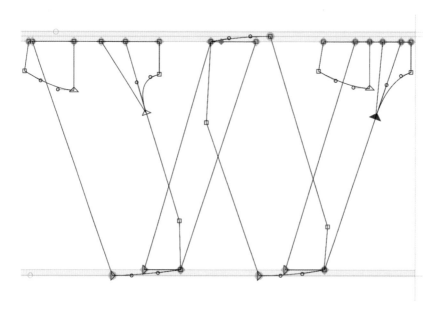

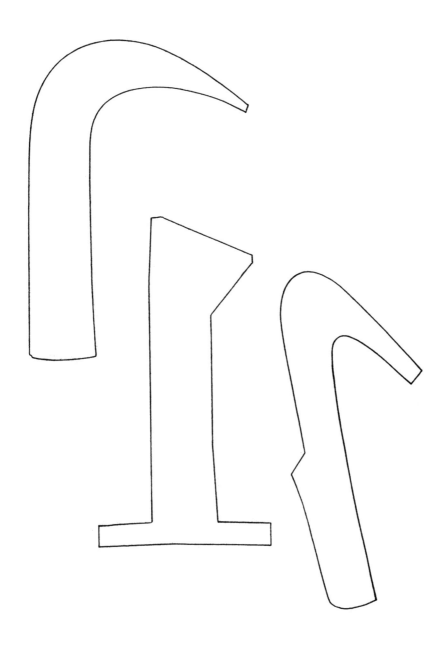

▲ Stencils of composite parts made by
William Addison Dwiggins for his *Falcon*,
1961, Linotype. Reduced.
From: Dorothy Abbe, *Stencilled Ornament &
Illustration*, 1979, Püterschein-Hingham.

a b c d e f g h i j k l m n o p q r s ſ t u v x y z

Æ æ ɑ & ff ffi fi ffl fl œ ſi ſl ſſ ffi ſt ꝰ á à â ã ç é è

ë ê ę í ì î ï ñ ó ò ô õ ꝑ ꝓ ꝑ ꝗ ꝗ ꝗ ꝗ ú ù û ü ú

1 2 3 4 5 6 7 8 9 0 . : , ; ! ? (| - * ¶ §

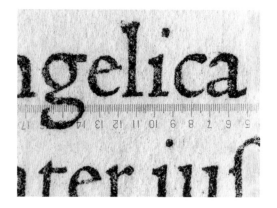

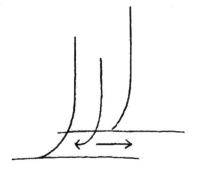

Doubts have been raised about whether she was a real historical personage or merely a fictional creation.

⏚ Hendrik van den Keere, *Small Pica Roman* (9 p. Didot), *c.* 1580. Actual size.
From: Hendrik D.L. Vervliet, *Sixteenth-Century Printing Types of the Low Countries*, 1968, Menno Hertzberger & Co.

▲ Traces of the broad-nibbed pen in the foot serifs of Nicolas Jenson's roman, following the scribe's way of making a bilateral serif without lifting the pen. The ruler is in millimetres. Enlarged.
PHOTO: RICCARDO OLOCCO

▲ *Diotima*, 1951–1953, Stempel.

10 Structure, pattern, texture

The structure of a typeface, its floor plan, primarily consists of the proportions underpinning a design: the ratios between x-height, capital height and total height, the position of the baseline and x-height within the total height, an average width for all signs (normal, condensed, wide), as well as the relative widths of individual characters (**l**, **n**, **m**). This structure supports the main parts of the typographic signs such as stems, large curves, diagonals, and horizontal parts. However, designers often follow a different path: after a sketching phase, burgeoning letterforms are measured for an underlying structure, while the vertical and horizontal proportions and the major parts of letters can still be mutually adapted.

When punches were cut by hand, one of the ways to capture an underlying structure was to create gauges with the main proportions, for the x-height, the size of the capitals, and for ascenders and descenders. Then punchcutters could start cutting and digging, using counter punches, files and burins.[1] The gauges were used to check and compare results for consistency and coherence. Fundamentally, type designers still work in a similar way after setting up the basic proportions for a type design, though we do not cut, dig and chip away anymore, but move control points, pull at handles, smooth curves and transitions from curves to straight parts, etc, shaping letterforms until they work together well.

The x-height is the most important of the basic proportions – more important than the total height.[a] When typefaces are visually evaluated, they must be compared with equal x-heights. Typefaces can have small or large x-heights within the total height of a design. A comparison on the basis of total height would give a false impression, making the typeface with a modest x-height look smaller than the one with a large x-height.

Old-face and modern-face configurations with, respectively, diagonal stress and gradual transitions from thick to thin, or vertical stress and more sudden transitions from thick to thin, are prominent features of

a] Type size, whether expressed in points as the total height of letters including ascenders and descenders, or in number of pixels for screens, does not mean much in relation to the experience of readers. As there are typefaces with large and small x-heights, the x-height is the primary measurement on which to base a notion of legibility. A typeface with a large x-height has, as a consequence, shorter ascenders and descenders than a face with a small x-height. If different typefaces are enlarged and reduced so that their x-heights are equal, their type sizes or total heights will be different.

many typefaces. It can be argued that these are not mere additions to the basic structure of a type design but are part of it, as they are the result of writing with specific tools. (Sanserifs often possess aspects of this structure, either having diagonal or vertical stress but with hardly any difference between thick and thin.) Serifs can be the subject of a similar discussion: are these intrinsic to the basic structure or are they attachments; are they part of Gill's body – bones and muscles – or are they clothes? [See chapter 5.]

In Roman Imperial capitals the serifs were not mere attachments. In *The Origin of the Serif* (1991, originally 1968) Edward M. Catich (1906–1979) showed that serifs are not the result of stone-cutting, of ending strokes in an elegant way with a chisel, but were painted by the Romans with a brush before cutting. They are short, sharp turns at the ends of strokes with some additional brushwork to complete foot serifs, for example.[2] Similarly in the Carolingian minuscule, as well as in some humanistic scripts, serifs are short, horizontal stroke-endings (although they also occur as separate strokes).[3]

Early in the fifteenth century, Roman square capitals were copied and adapted to cooperate with humanistic minuscules.[4] Later that century scribes began to add horizontal strokes to verticals along the baseline: foot serifs on the **f, h, i, l, m, n, p, q, r,** long **s,** and **x,** to make them 'blend more harmoniously with the recently adopted inscriptional majuscules'.[5] In making such an extension the pen was not lifted on reaching the baseline but was moved a little to the left and then to the right across the bottom of the vertical. These foot serifs are the result of connected writing movements. Often scribes were not consistent in applying this form of serif and mixed them with simple outgoing strokes or hooked terminals. The early creators of roman type, Johann (?–1469/70) & Wendelin (?–1477) von Speyer and especially Nicolas Jenson, applied foot serifs that clearly reflected the writing movements, and fixed the distribution of serifs that is still in use today.[b]

Foot serifs were subsequently simplified and made symmetrical by later punchcutters, probably to harmonize these with the serifs of the capitals. In some recent type designs, Jenson-like asymmetrical foot serifs have been reintroduced.

b] Hargreaves (1992), p 30. The symmetrical serifs of Jenson's capitals have a different origin: they reflect lapidary serifs the Renaissance humanists found in Roman inscriptions.

The criterion for being part of the basic structure may be: inherent, not acquired. In this sense, the main strokes of letterforms, a contrast between thick and thin, and also the serifs are structural phenomena. However, with the current way of making letterforms, often involving serifs as separate and customizable elements, serifs are no longer structural elements – a situation that actually applies to all parts of letters and other typographical signs. It appears that type design has become detached from the original, direct and organic way of shaping letters by writing, and is now more indirect and synthetic than ever. This does not seem to lead to a decline in type design – on the contrary, it results in a boundless adaptability and flexibility of letterforms.

Type designers can combine a high or low contrast, or something in between, with wide and round, or narrow and angular letterforms, with long or short ascenders and descenders, with large or modest capitals, with serifs or not – many combinations are possible. The repetition of any of such combinations in typeset text leads to the appearance of a pattern, which is bolstered by language.

Every written language has many character combinations – such as *the, ism* or *ough* in English – appearing regularly in a written text. Such groups of letters are parts of constantly recurring sequences of words, of the customary combinations of nouns and adjectives, of subjects and predicates, of the positions of adverbs, prepositions, etc. – in short: grammar and syntax. Clearly a seriffed typeface with a high contrast will make a different pattern than a low-contrast design without serifs. Changes to a type design, even small ones, influence a pattern, as any change is repeated often in a typeset text. And different languages, such as Dutch, French, Italian, Finnish, each affect the pattern brought about by a type design.

When a text is set in a large typesize, say with an x-height of 2.5 mm, the pattern of the typeface shows itself clearly. Below an x-height of approximately 1.5 mm, many details of a type design are less visible at normal reading distance (around 40 cm) and the pattern will change into a texture, often referred to by typographers as the 'colour' of a typeset text. Here colour means tonal value, which is determined by the relative weights of parts of a typeface, by the amounts of space that come with each sign, by the complexity or simplicity of a type design. It is a blend of black (or another colour) with the background colour in and around the letters.

The difference between pattern and texture is limited; it is mainly a matter of scale, of the size of a text and of the distance from reader to text. Many details that are easily discernible in large sizes can still be noticed in small sizes, but then you really have to pay attention while you are reading. And although a text for immersive reading will decidedly manifest itself as a texture, readers probably still perceive many distinguishing features that are more clearly visible in large sizes.

1. Smeijers (1996), pp 75–82, and 101–103.
2. Catich (1991), pp 220–225.
3. Knight (1998), pp 50–59, 89.
4. Ullman (1960), pp 54–56; Hargreaves (1992), pp 25, 26.
5. Twomey (1989), p 139; see also Hargreaves (1992), p 26.

xNhpé1Ijlnm

hxyhxyhxy

▲ The structure of a typeface, its floor plan, primarily consists of the proportions underpinning a design: the ratios between x-height, capital height and total height, the position of the baseline and x-height within the total height, an average width for all signs (normal, condensed, wide), as well as the relative widths of individual characters (**l**, **n**, **m**).

▲ Left: *Capitolium* regular, 60 point, centre: *Capitolium Headline* regular, 60 point, right: *Capitolium Headline* regular, 51 point, reduced to the same x-height as *Capitolium* regular, 60 point. Gerard Unger, *Capitolium*, 1998, TypeTogether.

▶ Serifs reflecting writing movements in Nicolas Jenson's roman. Enlarged.

▲ '... short sharp turns at the end of strokes with some additional brushwork ...'. Serifs as connected writing movements of Roman square capitals.
From: Edward M. Catich, *The Origin of the Serif*, 1991, St. Ambrose University.

Pattern theory is a distinctive approach to the analysis of all forms of real-world signals. At its core is the design of a large variety of probabilistic models whose samples reproduce the look and feel of the real signals, their patterns, and their variability. Bayesian statistical inference then allows you to apply these models in the analysis of new signals.

Pattern theory is a distinctive approach to the analysis of all forms of real-world signals. At its core is the design of a large variety of probabilistic models whose samples reproduce the look and feel of the real signals, their patterns, and their variability. Bayesian statistical inference then allows you to apply these models in the analysis of new signals.

Taal is in het algemeen elke min of meer complexe vorm van communicatie in de vorm van tekens, die gezamenlijk een systeem vormen. De term kan daarbij betrekking hebben op het systeem als geheel waarvan de tekens de individuele bouwstenen vormen, of op slechts een of enkele van de tekens afzonderlijk.

Le langage est la capacité d'exprimer une pensée et de communiquer au moyen d'un système de signes (vocaux, gestuel, graphiques, tactiles, olfactifs, etc.) doté d'une sémantique, et le plus souvent d'une syntaxe – mais ce n'est pas systématique (la cartographie est un exemple de langage non syntaxique). Fruit d'une acquisition, la langue est une des nombreuses manifestations du langage.

Il linguaggio, in linguistica, è il complesso definito di suoni, gesti e movimenti attraverso il quale si attiva un processo di comunicazione. La facoltà di rappresentare mentalmente un significato è presente in molte specie di animali, tra le quali l'essere umano.

Kieli on järjestelmä, jossa ihminen ilmaisee ajatuksensa kielellisillä merkeillä, abstraktioilla. Näitä merkkejä nimitetään kielellisiksi ilmauksiksi. Puhutuissa kielissä kuuluvia (auditiivisia) merkkejä tuotetaan puhe-elimillä. Kirjoitetussa kielessä kielelliset ilmaukset on tehty silmin nähtäviksi eli luettaviksi.

▲ A seriffed typeface with a high contrast makes a different pattern than a low-contrast design without serifs.

▲ Different languages, such as Dutch, French, Italian, Finnish, each affect the pattern brought about by a type design. *BigVesta Pro*, Linotype.

We construct the world around us by continually making observations about what we see. An observation is a phenomenon that can be witnessed and recorded. A set of observations can be used to make a hypothesis, which is a possible explanation for the observations made, but note a hypothesis is just a possible explanation. Sometimes, we get new evidence from an experiment or new observations that contradict our hypothesis. An experiment is a procedure carefully done to examine the validity of a hypothesis. In fact, scientists seek to test their hypotheses by making extensive observations or conducting many experiments. The idea is to prove a hypothesis by trying to disprove it first. A hypothesis can be changed or reformulated over a series of observations or experiments. Once a hypothesis holds true, it is accepted as fact.

Over the course of time, a collection of hypotheses can be used to generate either a scientific law or theory. A scientific law is a statement that summarizes a collection of observations or results from experiments. Scientific laws are always true under the same conditions and therefore can be used to make predictions. In fact, our cartoon friend here could use some of the Laws of Inheritance to better understand why some cats are gray, while other cats are orange, black, white, or even calico! In case you've never heard of them, the Laws of Inheritance were developed by the Austrian monk Gregor Mendel to explain inheritance patterns initially observed in pea plants. Collectively, the laws explain how genes are passed from parents to their offspring.

▲ When a text is set in a large typesize, say with an x-height of 2.5 mm, the pattern of the typeface shows itself clearly. Below an x-height of approximately 1.5 mm, many details of a type design are less visible at normal reading distance (around 40 cm) and the pattern will change into a texture, often referred to by typographers as the 'colour' of a typeset text. Left: *Flora*, 1984, Hell, right: *Portada*, 2016, TypeTogether.

11 Consistency and coherence

Consistency works on two levels: within a font and between the fonts or variants of a type family. Within a single font and across all the fonts of a type design it is the consistent application, interpretation, and harmonious co-operation of all character parts which creates coherence and significantly contributes to the formation of a well behaved group of letters. For readers using hand-held devices, such as books, magazines or tablets displaying substantial amounts of text in a small size – say, several paragraphs with an x-height of about 1.5 mm – it is enjoyable and even desirable when they can read smoothly. Consistency within a font and the coherence of a type family can make a significant contribution to this experience.

Elements that help to build consistency by receiving similar treatment are, for example: stem width, lengths of ascenders and descenders, curve conduct, terminals, serif formation, the distribution of space, and more. Such elements can and should be treated similarly, although some components need not or cannot always be dealt with in exactly the same way; the curved underside of a letter c, for instance, should look similar to that of the e and the t, but in the e it is stretched somewhat because an e is often a little wider than a c. On the t this curve is compressed. Many details have to be interpreted in similar ways, while maintaining consistency.

This process can be taken a step further: details that can get a similar treatment do not always need to be given a similar shape. The top right terminals of c and r can both be ball shaped, or the c can have a serif-like ending and the r more of a flag-like and flared ending. With balancing the weights of such divergent details, or by bringing them as close together in shape as is possible, consistency remains intact. This means that such subtle inconsistencies, if that is what they are, can be covered up or camouflaged. This kind of variation can also be regarded as diversity within consistency or convention. On the basis of conventional shapes of letters, there is a choice of known and tried solutions for details; just as there are several conventional shapes for letters, for example e and e, details have conventional variations as well.

Type designers can go further yet and introduce unconventionalities while applying these consistently. For example, an unusually flat top for the A and for the undersides of V and W can be combined with similar solutions for k, K, v,

V, **w**, **W**, **x**, **X**, **y** and **Y**, and possibly for **M** and **N**, and for a few more letters and signs. Applying such unusual details on the widest possible scale in a type design restores consistency to a certain extent. Even pronounced inconsistencies or disharmonies, as for example in *Horseferry* (2015) designed by Brody Associates for Channel 4 Television (UK), can become consistent to a degree.[a] Here, too, language lends a hand with the regular repetition of frequent character combinations, customary word order, and so on.

a] The complete credit is: *Horseferry* designed by Brody Associates at the request of 4Creative, the in-house creative agency of Channel 4.

Although repetition of marked inconsistencies in a typeface throughout a text restores consistency and coherence to a certain extent, the appearance of a text can nevertheless be unconventional.

Consistency between the members of a type family and the coherence of a group of fonts largely corresponds to that within a font. Details of the regular weight are carried over to the lighter and heavier versions – which usually is not a straightforward operation. If, for example, the regular has a moderate difference between thick and thin parts, then this contrast increases when versions get heavier and decreases when they are made lighter. Partly these are optical adjustments, of which there are many to be made in a type design [see chapter 13]. If, in a black or ultra-heavy version, the **a**, **e** and **s** have to look similar to those in the regular, all horizontal parts need to be thinner in relation to the thick parts than in the regular; otherwise the counters, the spaces within the letters, will become too small and will make these letters look too dark. A comparison of *Zeitung* (2016) light and black, by Underware, shows how this can be done: in this type design not only some horizontal parts of the black version have been visibly thinned, the top right part of the **e**, for example, has been made lighter as well.[b]

b] In Eric Gill's ultra-bold version (1931/2) of *Gill Sans* (1928) similar distortions or corrections can be observed. http://www.underware.nl/blog/2016/11/new-font-zeitung/ (21/04/2017).

The small interior spaces of heavy variants of a type design make it difficult to fit properly, to balance correctly the spaces within and between the characters [see chapter 14]. Some spaces between several combinations of letters, such as *wt* in pewter or *vvy* in chivvying, will make for more marked gaps in bolds and blacks than in the regular and lighter versions – another hurdle in guaranteeing consistency among weights.

A type design with a high contrast in the regular is easier to make as a black version than a monolinear design. Light versions of the latter are relatively easy to keep open, while in heavy monolinear versions many characters such as **g**, **§**, **4** and **8** (as well as **a**, **e** and **s**) end up as highly adapted versions of the regular forms, again because of the risk of tiny interior spaces. To make the thin versions of a design (thinner than the light) look like next of kin of the ultra black, both with distinct family traits, many parts and combinations of parts have to be adjusted in all fonts while maintaining consistency as much as possible. As a consequence of many adjustments, the extreme versions (very light and very black) can grow too far apart, and so sometimes interpolation requires an intermediate version, such as a semi-bold, to generate weights between this version and a thin, and between the semi-bold and an ultra black.

Arapaima
Avadavat
Ataraxia

High in the branches
of the Great Oak,
the hooded man silently
draws an arrow from
the quiver strapped across
his back and notches it to
the string of his bow.

▲ Lee Yuen-Rapati, *Matic*, 2017. MA Typeface Design of the University of Reading. A type design with a flat-topped A and similar solutions for other characters, inspired by mid-twentieth-century typography on wristwatches.

▲ Brody Associates, *Horseferry*, 2015, designed for Channel 4.

113

Channel4
Our twin goals as a content provider and business are to fulfil our remit and **to be commercially self-sufficient.**

Our twin goals as a content provider **and business are to fulfil our remit and** to be commercially self-sufficient.
Channel 4

When creating horizontal parts, such as beams, **always pick points in the same direction.**

For example, pick positions from left to right, and from bottom to top.

▲ Brody Associates, *Horseferry* (left) and its companion typeface *Chadwick* (right), 2015, designed for Channel 4.

▲ *Zeitung* light and black, 2016, Underware. In the black some horizontal parts have been drastically thinned, and the top right part of the e, for example, has been lightened.

12 Rhythm and space

A simple writing exercise explains the working of rhythm and space in a type design. Take up a pen, make a diagonal upstroke, a vertical downstroke, and repeat this several times without lifting pen or pencil from paper, while keeping the same distance between the vertical downstrokes. Bringing these closer together or increasing the distance between them changes the spaces and the rhythm. In its simplicity this exercise touches upon one of the main concerns of the type designer: forming rhythmical lines of text with as even a distribution of space as possible within and between all typographic signs.

When the verticals and diagonals of the exercise above are joined by curves and horizontal segments, both large and small, and parts such as the right side of the **k**, the inter-character spaces become varied in shape. It is still possible to arrive at a regular cadence by balancing all these spaces, both within and between characters, and bringing them as close together in area as possible [see chapter 14], while keeping the inter-character spaces slightly smaller in area than the interior spaces. In general the rule is: the smaller the type size, the wider both the signs and the spaces between them should be, and the reverse goes for the larger sizes [see chapter 17].

Different rhythms are at work in type designs: an old-face rhythm, which lasted till well into the eighteenth century, and a modern-face rhythm, which is a late eighteenth- and especially a nineteenth-century development. In old face (with diagonal stress) letters such as **a**, **e**, **s**, **R** or **S** are rather slim, while characters like **b**, **d**, **O**, **M** and **Z** are often wide. Near the end of the eighteenth century a tendency towards equal width of letterforms emerged with the modern face (vertical stress), and wide characters like **m**, **M**, **o**, **O**, **w** and **W** were compressed while narrow characters such as **a**, **e**, **s** or **S** were widened.[a] On top of this development all characters were equally condensed in the course of the nineteenth century, with a lattice-like effect in lines of text as a consequence, accentuated by the thin horizontal and thick vertical parts [see chapter 4].

a] Updike (1962) II, pp 171, 194, 197 and illustration nr. 327 between pp 186 and 187. Of course the narrowest characters such as i, j, l, or 1 cannot be condensed.

The tendency towards equal width can be found already earlier in the eighteenth century, for example in the type specimen of Pierre-Simon Fournier le jeune from 1766, in his famous *Cicéro, gros œil, dans le goût Hollandois*. This design shows, with other faces cut by Fournier, that condensing is one of the causes of the tendency towards equal width. Otherwise Fournier's letterforms were transitional, with some letters already showing vertical stress and others still having diagonal stress.[1]

The old-face rhythm made a massive comeback at the end of the nineteenth and throughout the twentieth century, with many type designs based on historical, seriffed models. The tendency towards equal width made an equally massive comeback with sanserifs like *Helvetica* (1957) and *Univers* (1957), both based on the structure of the modern face.[b] Thereafter the tendency towards equal width has also appeared in many seriffed type designs. This influence increased so much towards the end of the twentieth century (and even more in the early part of the twenty-first century) that it has led to a 'model of the early twenty-first century': fairly condensed seriffed typefaces with a moderate contrast and often short and stubby serifs, designs that are economical, work well on screens, on illuminated backgrounds, and remain intact at low resolutions,[c] such as *Bree Serif* (2013) and *Portada* (2016), both designed by Veronika Burian (1973–) and José Scaglione (1974–).

b] These sanserifs, and also *Akzidenz Grotesk*, basically have modern-face attributes, while an equally famous sanserif like *Gill Sans* is based on the old-face structure.

c] Low resolutions hardly play a role anymore as resolutions on screens now are generally high enough to display letterforms faithfully, for example with Retina displays from 2012.

With the publication of Adrian Frutiger's *Avenir* in 1988, the tendency towards equal width also became associated with geometric sanserifs – or rather with the fusion of geometric sans, Grotesque and humanist sanserif, as described above [see chapter 7]. Since then many designs have been made that come close to *Avenir*, most of which show the tendency towards equal width, often with all characters widened equally, including **a**, **e** and **s**.[d]

d] For example *Proxima Nova* (2005) by Mark Simonson.

---

1. Fournier (1995), p 40.

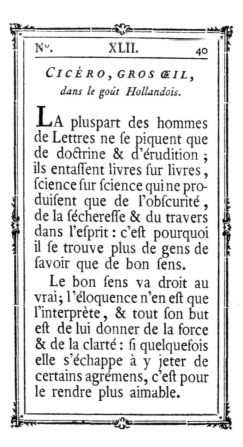

If you'd like your sand castle to remain intact, I suggest you build it away from the water.

▲ Pierre-Simon Fournier le jeune, Cicéro Gros Œil, dans le goût Hollandois, c. 1766. Actual size.
From: *The Manuel Typographique of Pierre-Simon Fournier le jeune*, 1995, Technische Hochschule Darmstadt.

▲ *Bree Serif*, 2013, TypeTogether.

If contrast level
is being manipulated into
higher contrast levels
relative to the
original painting,
then the moderate
contrast condition
**should result in higher
appreciation than
the high contrast
condition.**

▲ *Portada*, 2016, TypeTogether.

13 Optical adjustments

If all the letters and parts of letters that have the same height as the **x** (for example **a, c, e, o** and the curved parts of **b** and **d**) appear to be equally high, they have been optically adjusted.[a] This too is an essential factor in creating group behaviour and consistency. For instance, the curved top and bottom parts of the **o** should protrude slightly above and below the x-height – or the **o** would seem to be too small. There are many such adjustments: for example, where two diagonals meet they are often tapered to prevent the occurrence of a dark spot in a text; or, when a type design should look monolinear, the horizontal parts can be made slightly thinner than the vertical parts, otherwise they would seem too heavy; and so on. Such adjustments are, of course, also applied to capitals, numerals, and all other typographic signs.[1]

a] Hochuli (2005), p 18. Jost Hochuli is of the opinion that optical adjustments occur so much in letterforms and equally frequently in many other visible everyday things that he rather speaks of optical facts – meaning they are self-evident.

With such adjustments, a string of letters is properly aligned and text looks smooth; yet the question remains as to whether such corrections can be calculated or whether they are a matter for an individual designer's optical judgement. The latter is the most likely, and the most common approach, since it depends on each design concept how far curves should extend (overshoot) above and below the horizontal guidelines, for example: very round or circular curves extend further above and below the **x** than flat curves.

In italics the stems of **b**, **d** and **f** often need to be optically aligned by putting the **f** slightly upright in comparison with **b** and **d**. Depending on the design, the curved parts at the top and bottom may seem to increase the slope of the **f** and make it look as if it leans more to the right than **b** and **d**. There are many similar adjustments to be made.

The final version of *Futura* (1927) shows many optical adjustments to prevent text from looking spotty, 'subtle design features that gave the appearance of true geometric letterforms'.[2] This means that the geometry of *Futura* was more sophisticated than that of the lowercase-only design (1926) by Herbert Bayer, which was 'geometrically constructed with the minimum use of arcs and angles'.[b] The geometric refinements of *Futura* were deliberately removed by Remco van Bladel (1977–) for a book about the Dutch

b] Spencer (1968), p 59. In addition to the design by Herbert Bayer from 1926 there was also a geometric and strictly monolinear design by Jan Tschichold from 1930. See: Burke (2007), pp.154–6.

artist Herman de Vries (1931–). Because the work of De Vries is based on elements from nature, this variation of *Futura* has been named *Natura* (also lowercase only, 2015), and is based on early drawings for *Futura*, which contained
many of the unconventional letterforms that were later offered by the Bauer
typefoundry as alternatives.[3] In fact, these early drawings show letterforms
that are practically monolinear.

While more purely monolinear type designs have been made, such as
Variex (c. 1988) by Zuzana Licko and Rudy Vanderlans (1955–), in some type
designs the horizontal parts have deliberately been made heavier than
the vertical elements, as was done rather subtly in *Antique Olive* (1962–
1966) by Roger Excoffon [see chapter 7]. Thus, optical adjustments or the premeditated absence of these, or deliberate changes in the conventional
distribution of thick and thin parts of letterforms, can all lead to well-func-
tioning type designs, if consistently apportioned. And even if weight
is partially inconsistent, as in *Keedy Sans* (c. 1989) by Jeffery Keedy (1957–),
then language will help to restore consistency somewhat [see chapters 11 and 15],
and allow the font to function reasonably well.

1. L. Meseguer, in Henestrosa (2017), pp 69–72.
2. Burke (1998), p 89.
3. Burke (1998), pp 87, 88, 103.

Squirrels cannot digest cellulose, so they must rely on foods rich in protein, carbohydrates, and fats. In temperate regions, early spring is the hardest time of year for squirrels, because buried nuts begin to sprout and are no longer available for the squirrel to eat, and new food sources have not become available yet. During these times, squirrels rely heavily on the buds of trees. Squirrels' diets consist primarily of a wide variety of plants, including nuts, seeds, conifer cones, fruits, fungi, and green vegetation.

however, some squirrels also consume meat, especially when faced with hunger. squirrels have been known to eat insects, eggs, small birds, young snakes, and smaller rodents. indeed, some tropical species have shifted almost entirely to a diet of insects. predatory behavior has been noted by various species of ground squirrels, in particular the thirteen-lined ground squirrel. for example, bailey, a scientist in the 1920s, observed a thirteen-lined ground squirrel preying upon a young

▲ Left: *Futura*, right: *Natura*

XO

dfb *influx*

dfb *influx*

aa

⬆ The curved top and bottom parts of the **o** protrude slightly above and below the x-height.

⬆ Compared with the **f** above, the one below is put slightly upright to make it align optically with the **d** and **b**.

▲ Right: the **a** of *Futura* medium, 1927, with refinements; left: the **a** of *Natura*, 2015, without.

altogether completely entirely essentially exactly exclusively

These plants prefer full sun or partial shade.

▲ *Variex*, c. 1988, Emigre.   ▲ *Keedy Sans*, c. 1989, Emigre.

14 Fitting

Fitting is allocating the amounts of space on both sides of each character in a font so that in any combination, in all words and lines of text, the inter-character spaces are well-balanced with their internal spaces, and so that the characters 'have a balanced relationship, without unsightly gaps or congestion'.[1] The spaces on the left and right of metal letterforms were called sidebearings, a term that can be used for digital typography as well. Fitting can be seen as part of optical adjusting, but it is an operation in itself.

This part of type design is sometimes called spacing or letter-spacing (which is also called tracking), but those terms denote the increasing or decreasing of spaces between characters, apart from the amounts of space they were already given by fitting.

Fitting usually begins with the lowercase **n** and **o**. The **o** is one of the few symmetrical (and fairly frequent)[a] characters in a seriffed type design with equal spaces on each side, apart from the **v**, **w**, **x** and **z**, which are less easily fitted; **i** and **l** in sanserif designs are usually symmetrical, but they have no internal spaces. There are symmetrical capitals as well, but these have to wait their turn; lowercase letters come first as they are most common in text.

a] In the English language the o takes up approximately 7.5% of a text, the n 6.74%, the e 12.7%, and the t 9%. See: https://en.wikipedia.org/wiki/Letter_frequency (17/09/2017).

An **n** is slightly asymmetrical, having a curve on the upper right and the top of a stem on the left. When the **n**, whether seriffed or sanserif, is placed between two **o**'s and the spaces between these three letters are balanced so that the two sidebearings of the **n** added together amount to a little less than the space within the **n**, then you have a good starting point for further fitting.

The spaces of the **n** are applied to the **m**, to the **h** (with a small adjustment on the left as there is no serif at the top of the x-height but high up on the ascender) and to the **i** and **l** and **u** (also with small adjustments). The spaces for the **c**, **d**, **e**, **p**, **q**, **r** can be derived from those of the **o** and **n**, while comhuminim ilimodomcumidim inemopomquh and similar combinations, and real words and sentences, enable comparison and fine tuning of the inter-character spaces. Next, **a**, **f**, **g**, **s**, **t**, **v** and the other letters are added; capitals are fitted to work with the lowercase; punctuation, numerals, and all other signs in a font join in. This procedure is the same for seriffed designs and sanserifs. Often designers have their own variations for these procedures.

Rules for fitting were fairly elementary for metal type, while digital type allows for many subtleties. However, perfection is unattainable: a proper fitting will always end up as a compromise. The shapes of letters and other signs are so diverse and are combined in so many ways in different languages that a perfect balancing act is impossible. Especially in the heavier weights, satisfactory fitting is hard to achieve because of the often small amounts of space within letters: the counters of the **w** are very small while the diagonal parts prevent it from getting close to many other letters, whereas **h**, **i** or **l** can be fitted compactly, as in the word while. Nevertheless, reasonably good fitting is accepted and appreciated by readers; actually, this is one of the parts of a type design that readers are the least aware of, and which may only begin to interest or irritate them when the fitting is in bad shape. **b**

b] Tracy (1986) offers a useful method for the basic fitting of a Latin typeface; pp 70–80. Other texts on fitting and related subjects are: J. Blumenthal (1935). The fitting of type; W.A. Dwiggins (1940), *WAD to RR: a Letter about Designing Type*; F. Smeijers (1996), *Counterpunch*; L. De Groot (2015), *Kernologica*.

Letters such as **c** and **r** are tricky: in a type design with serifs the **c** will, when correctly fitted, seem to be too close to a following **n** and to keep some distance from an **o** next to it. Such optical illusions are caused by the serif on the top left of the **n** and the roundness of the **o**. Likewise, when the **n** and **o** are fitted satisfactorily and you set the word 'noon', the two o's seem to be too close together – again an optical illusion. Fitting means dealing with such illusions frequently. Generally, when **cn**, **co** or **oo** appear in words and in a line of text, in type sizes below 12 point, they look acceptable – e.g: financial, incoherent, cooperate.

The ultimate aim of fitting is to turn a text into a pattern or a texture [see chapter 10] with a regular alternation of dark and light elements, the main ingredient of which is the weight of vertical strokes: straight, curved, and diagonal. The parallel goal is to supply readers with an agreeable rhythm in text, neither too tightly fitted nor too wide [see chapter 12]. Again, the overarching priority is group behaviour, in this case of a neighbourly kind.

There will always be gaps left that cannot be bridged by basic fitting, for instance in the combinations **Ta**, **Tc** or **Te**, **Vo**, and others, mainly of **T**, **V**, **W** and **Y** with many lowercase letters, but also of a **w** with a full stop (w.), for instance. The spaces between such specific pairs of characters can be adjusted with kerning, mostly with negative space.

Many combinations of characters need special attention, such as **f** and **è** (French: fète). The overhanging part of the **f** may hit the accent above the **è** – then either this pair can be kerned (with extra space), the overhanging top of the **f** can be shortened, or the accents can be redesigned and angled more upright. Sometimes you have to accept large spaces between letters. In harvest it is possible to let the **r** and **v** overlap, but not too much or the **r** will lose its identity: harvest. And in revving, two **v**'s too close together will look like a **w**: revving. Spaces between letters should be tested in many different combinations and for many languages. If, for example, you have designed a handsome **g** with a generous lower loop, it is possible that in Italian or Dutch gg will stand out on a page or screen and may irritate readers: oggi, viaggio (Italian), bruggen, vlaggen (Dutch).

Capitals, which are primarily fitted to cooperate with lowercase, need to be spaced (tracked) when used in all-capital setting. In OpenType, capitals can be fitted to both cooperate with lowercase and to stand on their own. Likewise, numerals can be fitted optically like lowercase, as well as to occupy the same width for tabular setting – both ranging and non-ranging numerals. Such different spatial organizations for capitals and numerals are recent extensions of the grammar of legibility, expanding the possibilities for typographic designers to increase the comfort for readers [see chapter 3].

1. Tracy (1986), p 71.

Glyph:	n		n		c		n		n	
Width:	620		620		466		620		620	
Left:	41		41		43		41		41	
Right:	32		32		30		32		32	
Kerning:	0	nn	0	nc	0	cn	0	nn	0	

Glyph:	o		o		c		o		o	
Width:	564		564		466		564		564	
Left:	43		43		43		43		43	
Right:	43		43		30		43		43	
Kerning:	0	oo	0	oc	0	co	0	oo	0	

▲ Although correctly fitted, the c seems to be too close to the n and keeping a distance from the o. (Screenshot)

Glyph:	o	n	o
Width:	564	620	564
Left:	43	41	43
Right:	43	32	43
Kerning:	0 on	0 no	0

▲ The **n** fitted correctly between two **o**'s, with 41 units on the left and 32 on the right. (Screenshot)

Glyph:	T	o	n	n	o
Width:	541	626	637	637	626
Left:	10	52	69	69	52
Right:	10	52	63	63	52
Kerning:	0 To	-85 on	0 nn	0 no	0

Glyph:	T	o	n	n	o
Width:	541	626	637	637	626
Left:	10	52	69	69	52
Right:	10	52	63	63	52
Kerning:	0 To	0 on	0 nn	0 no	0

▲ Above: 'To' without kerning; below: with kerning (-85). (Screenshot)

15 Ideas of interference

The type designer's purpose usually is to bring order and regularity to a type design, with convention, structure, consistency, coherence, and rhythm as key resources. Nevertheless, it is challenging to try and find out how far one can go with introducing diversity or irregularities in combination with consistency, coherence, and rhythm, either on the level of individual letterforms within a font (*Horseferry*) [see chapter 15] or on the level of the type family.

Monospaced typefaces present a challenge to good rhythm: the extreme condensing of wide letters such as **M** and **W**, and a widening of space around the narrowest letters such as **I**, **i** and **l**, often equipped with lengthy serifs, makes the spaces between the letters suffer: these become irregular. However, as the letters are both aligned horizontally and vertically, a strong pattern more or less compensates for the irregular spaces. A different case is *Anisette* (1996), a display typeface designed by Jean François Porchez (1964–) with alternative letter-widths. The mixing of narrow and wide versions of the same letter disturbs the rhythm that readers are familiar with. For a display typeface this is an effective way to arouse curiosity and hold the attention.

As consistency and coherence have been challenged on the font level, so has the type family been taken to task. An example is *Knockout* (1994) by Jonathan Hoefler (1970–), a family of headline fonts originally designed for the American magazine *Sports Illustrated*. The fonts each have individual details, making them more nieces and nephews than sisters and brothers. Each font is clearly consistent, while their straightforwardness and an air of having been treated with compass and ruler gives the family coherence. The idea for such a loose family was based on a collection of sanserifs in early twentieth-century type specimens of American Type Founders, partly designed by Morris Fuller Benton.[1] *Knockout* was presented as an alternative to a tightly organized and highly systematized type family like *Univers* (1957) by Adrian Frutiger.

Another example shows an unorthodox approach to the relationship between roman and italic: *Téras* (2013), designed by Sebastian Losch (1988–). The romans begin at the light end with fully fledged serifs and end as a black sanserif. The light italic has no in- and outgoing upstrokes while the black does have these. Intermediate versions move in opposite directions, meeting half-way. Again, each font shows consistency, while coherence is maintained by the application of strong characteristics related to calligraphy in all the fonts. The concept of the font family has been challenged even further, as with *Twin* (2003), designed by Just van Rossum and Erik van Blokland for the cities of Minneapolis and St. Paul in the United States, with unusual versions such as *Twin Weird* and *Twin Loopy*, each consistent as fonts and harmonized with the other members of the family, which shows complete coherence.

After 1985, when digital type design became widespread, designers have attempted to partly undo well-known approaches to type design by introducing randomness and arbitrariness. One of the striking and truly random designs from that period is *Beowolf* (1990) [see chapter 8]. In a text set with this typeface the typographic pattern is gradually transformed as the contours of letterforms become increasingly deformed, while the structure of the letters and the text remains the same. A similar idea is the *Scratched Letter* (2003) by Hansje van Halem (1978–), in which letters have lost their sharp contours. This creates doubt in the reader, although reading is as effortless as with hard-edged letters. Such interferences are mostly based on personal ideas and only rarely on scientific research.

In a study of type design for children with low vision, Ann Bessemans (1983–) has tested deviations from the strict verticality in upright typefaces (romans), variations in widths of letters and inter-character spaces, an unusual distribution of thick and thin, and a varying x-height.[2] Of these modifications those with slightly wobbly verticals and with different letter-widths let the visually impaired children read easier. In 2005 Jeremy Tankard (1969–) published his *Kingfisher* typeface with nearly imperceptible wobbling of letters, about which he wrote: 'The theory is that character irregularities will, when the type is set, give the text a lively pattern, nothing startling, but with just enough interest to entice the eyes. Perhaps, today the irregularities of punchcutting, once lost to industrialization, could be reintroduced in an attempt to reinvigorate the reading experience.'[3] Ann Bessemans' research has confirmed his assumption.

'Variation in slant is a vital factor in legibility which must not be confined to the lowercase f ...' This is John Ryder (1917–2001), typographer, arguing for more irregularity in italics to improve their legibility.[4] His example is *Janson* italic, originally cut by Nicholas Kis in Amsterdam between 1680 and 1689.[5] As mentioned above, wobbliness in the roman does help some to read better; and because italic occurs less often than roman, and is therefore less subject to convention, it leaves more room for idiosyncrasies. However, it still has to be researched whether wobbliness will benefit more readers than young ones with impaired vision, both in roman and italic.

Distorted typefaces already appeared in the nineteenth century, sloping leftwards, broken or zigzagging, with horizontals as the heaviest parts of letters, and more [see chapter 7].[6] Since then the desire of type designers to challenge the established norms or conventions of type design has become an integral part of the profession. As Jonathan Barnbrook (1966–) once stated: 'Unlike many designers I think the world would be a really boring place if everything was perfectly designed. We need a clashing of visual styles, naivety and alien influences to keep design alive.'[7]

1. Cost (2011), pp 289–327.
2. Bessemans (2012), pp 308–328.
3. Tankard (2005), p 8.
4. Ryder (1979), pp 75–77.
5. Haiman (1983), Enclosure No. 1.
6. Gray (1976), pp 55, 57, 69, 113, 130.
7. This quotation was copied from a previous version of Jonathan Barnbrook's website.

A language dies only when the
last person who speaks it dies.
Or perhaps it dies when the
second-last person who speaks
it dies, for then there is no
one left to talk to. There is
nothing unusual about a single
language dying. Communities
have come and gone throughout
history, and with them their
language.

PASTIS MASTIKA
RAKI PASTIS
OUZO ARAK
SAMBUCA OUZO
ARAK RAKI

▲ A monospaced typeface: Jim Lyles, *Menlo*,   ▲ *Anisette*, 1996, Typofonderie.
2009, Apple Inc.

Coherent Consistent
Consistent Coherent Consistent Coherent
Consistent Coherent Coherent
Coherent Consistent Consistent Coherent
Consistent Coherent Coherent Consistent
Coherent Consistent Consistent
Consistent Consistent Coherent Consistent
Coherent Coherent Consistent
Consistent Coherent Consistent Consistent Coherent
Coherent Consistent Coherent

transform *transform*

transform *transform*

transform *transform*

transform ***transform***

▲ *Knockout*, 1994, Hoefler & Co.

▲ *Téras*, 2013.

▶ *Twin Formal, Twin Weird* and *Twin Loopy*, 2003.

abcdefghi abcdefghi
jklmnopqr jklmnopqr
stuvwxyz stuvwxyz

ABCDEFGHIJ
KLMNOPQR
STUVWXYZ

ABCDEFGHIJ
KLMNOPQR
STUVWXYZ

abcdefgHI
jklmnopqr
stuvwxyz

Split rod for fixing the hooks of
the longline, 1850-1900
Split rod for fixing the hooks of
the longline, 1850-1900
Net-mending chest of J.J. Dorland
Czn, Marken, 1910
Net-mending chest, 1844
Bin with net-mending tools,
1850-1900
Chest with net-mending tools,
1850-1900
Tobacco tin with knitting needles,
paddles and fishing leads, 1900-1950
Net-mending tools, 1850-1950
Cigar box with net mending paddles,
1900-1950

Sailmaker
\> to #186: J. Max Sailmaking
Company, Amsterdam, 1850-1900
179-181 Sailmaker's hammer, 1850-1900
182 Sailmaker's hammer, 1900-1930
183, 184 Sailmaker's hammer, 1900-1950
185, 186 Sailmaker's hammer, 1850-1900
187 Sailmaker's rod, 1930
188 Sailor's palm, 1950
189 Grease horn with needles, 1850-1900
190 Samples book with canvas samples,
1961
191 Calendar of J. Max Sailmaking
Company, Amsterdam, 1954
192 Name strip of J. Max Sailmaking
Company, Amsterdam, 1950

▲ *Scratched Letter*, 2003
From: *NIJVER|heden, De evolutie van ambachten*, 2011,
Zuiderzeemuseum

Maarten Kolk Polder Data, 2008 Herbarium, 2006

For the **Veldwerk** (Fieldwork) project, Maarten Kolk (1980) made an inventory of the flora and fauna of the Noordoostpolder (North-east Polder, The Netherlands). Kolk used Rianne Makkink and Jurgen Bey's designer-in-residence workshop in the Noordoostpolder as the operating base for this study, which culminated in a book and a herbarium (collection of dried plants). The book deals with Kolk's study of the Noordoostpolder, illustrating the development of the area's vegetation along a visual timeline. The Noordoostpolder is particularly suitable for this type of study because its 'point zero' is relatively recent, which makes it possible to make a precise reconstruction of the historical development of the landscape from the start (in 1936) right down to the present. Except for the polders, there are no areas left in the Netherlands where this is still possible. The timeline, which runs from 1936 to 2007, consists of hand-stamped drawings of plants and animals. The density of the stamps indicates how commonly a specific animal or plant occurred in a particular period. In fact, this representation can be read like a graph; for example the mice plague of 1938 shows up on the timeline like a dark spot (of very densely placed mouse stamps!). Maarten Kolk also collected local plants which he dried, pressed and stored in a herbarium, showing the historic development of the Noordoostpolder vegetation.

Imagine time flowing in the pattern and trim the peak of the character's liveliness and excitement. Along the axis of time in the pattern, think, "Which scene best express the most lively scene."

Handzeichnungen von Pablo Picasso

▲ *Kingfisher*, 2005, Jeremy Tankard Typography.

▲ *Janson* italic, 1937, Stempel.

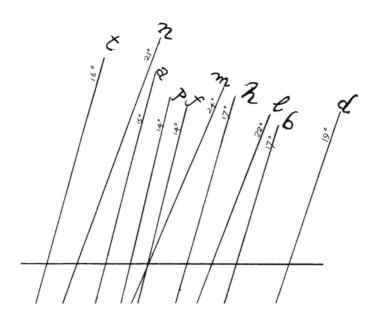

▲ John Ryder's slant analysis of *Janson* italic.
From: John Ryder, *The Case for Legibility*, 1979, The Bodley Head.

▲ Figgins, 1845, Two-line english *Zig-zag no. 1* and *no. 2*. Reduced.
From: Nicolete Gray, *Nineteenth Century Ornamented Typefaces*, 1976, Faber and Faber.

16 Italic

All that has been written so far about structure, pattern, texture, consistency, coherence, rhythm, space, and interferences by designers not only applies to romans from thin to ultra black, but also to italic in all its variations. However, italic has some properties of its own. Basically there are two concepts for italic: the true italic, evolved out of a kind of informal and fast writing developed in the early 1400s in Florence,[1] and the inclined or oblique roman.[a] An oblique roman is easily created electronically or digitally, but will show many distortions that need to be edited. Well designed oblique or slanted romans have become common alongside geometric or neo-grotesque sanserifs (*Futura*, 1927, *Helvetica*, 1957, *Avenir*, 1988), whereas sanserifs with an old-face structure, such as *Gill Sans* (1928), are mostly accompanied by a true italic with little contrast.

a] Morison (1926), pp 93–129. Slanted romans were used much earlier than the twentieth century. In the outer wall of the Frauenkirche in Munich, Germany, there is an inscription with text in a sloped roman, dated 1733.

Before it got this far, italic or cursive went through a lengthy process of adjustment to roman. The first Italic type cut in 1501 by Francesco Griffo for Aldus Manutius was lowercase only, combined with roman capitals.[2] In its early stages italic lowercase was sometimes pulled upright, as in Italy in 1554,[3] supposedly to harmonize it with the roman capitals, although calligraphers had already often used such a 'cancelleresca formata'. The first time capitals were sloped or italicized was around 1524.[4]

For a long time italics remained independent of roman, with the famous italics of Robert Granjon, around the middle of the sixteenth century 'probably the last to be envisaged as type for texts rather than as auxiliaries to Roman (sic)'.[5] Pierre-Simon Fournier le jeune made adjustments around 1742 with 'the introduction of roman serifs on lowercase letters such as **m, n, p** and **r**'.[6] This process of adaptation was taken further by François-Ambroise Didot and his punchcutter Pierre-Louis Vafflard around 1783.

Meanwhile, around the middle of the sixteenth century, italic was given its role as an auxiliary to roman, for 'a change of texture' and 'distinction rather than emphasis'.[7] For this kind of differentiation, and for emphasis as well, it is possible to make 'integrated distinctions' and 'active distinctions'.[8] Integrated distinctions mainly concern italics, while active distinctions mostly involve bold weights. Interestingly a 'negative active distinction' is the possibility to set a few words in regular within a bold text. Also for integrated distinctions other typefaces can be used, such as scripts.

Italic is mostly a little lighter in weight and narrower than roman, with a stronger rhythm and often with sharper curves, and usually with in-and out-going upstrokes instead of serifs; as shown, serifs can be found at the ends of straight parts. The angle of inclination of italics can vary from almost upright to about 20°.[b] Features of italic such as transitions from thin to thick, and connections between curves and stems, are usually harmonized and coordinated with those of the roman for coherence.

Nowadays an italic can be closely associated with a roman or may be less dependent. There are italics that differ substantially from the roman they have to work together with, such as *Galliard* italic (1978) designed by Matthew Carter after a typeface cut by Robert Granjon – a revival from the time that italics were still independent.

Roman and italic are now so closely associated that italics are hardly ever identified with typefaces related to handwriting, although italics can be seen as a group within the class of script typefaces. Scripts are type designs derived from studied writing, showing the influences of writing instruments such as pencils, pens, different kinds of brushes – any instrument that can be turned into a writing tool – sometimes quite emphatically, and often with fluid movements as a consequence of rapid writing.[c] Some script typefaces have letters that connect to each other, or cleverly seem to do so, as in Nicole Dotin's (1974) *Pique* (2014). But the letterforms of italics, like those of romans, are generally not joined. Yet, despite all the adjustments of italic to roman, italics have remained closer to their written ancestors than romans. If italics can be seen as scripts, then scripts can be considered as italics, giving type designers room to experiment with the tandem of roman and italic. Underware has done this with three italics for their *Auto* sanserif (2014), from a straightforward to a very lively version.

Incidentally, since italic is used to make clear to readers that they have to pay extra attention, any typeface capable of performing the same role and sufficiently different from a roman can be used for this purpose instead of italic, such as a light condensed variant. Gothic (blackletter) typefaces were almost never accompanied by an italic. For texts set in Fraktur, the common text type in Germany until World War Two, emphasis was achieved by spacing instead of italic.[d]

Designers have experimented recently again with autonomous italics, even as a family of italics only.[e] And between true italics and sloped romans designers have positioned hybrids: part sloped roman with serifs, mixed with true italic letterforms such as **a** and **e**. Examples are *Joanna* italic (1930–31) by Eric Gill

b] The italic of the typeface called *Old Style* has an inclination of 27°. It was cut by Alexander Phemister and published in 1860 by Miller & Richard in Edinburgh. The italic of *Romanée* (1949) by Jan van Krimpen and of *Trinité* (1982) by Bram de Does are nearly upright.

c] Max Caflisch, Swiss typographer and author, has attempted to classify scripts: Von Skripten, in: *Typografische Monatsblätter*, Nr. 6, 1996.

d] In 1941 Fraktur was outlawed by the Nazis. See Burke (1998), pp 165–167.

e] Such a family was designed in 2009 by Naïma Ben Ayed when she was a student at the École Estienne in Paris.

and *Trump Medieval* italic (1954) by Georg Trump (1896–1985). Such a variation can be put upright, as a member of a type family in its own right called 'informal'.[f] This variant is a recent addition to the typographic repertoire, to the grammar of legibility, and it offers new possibilities for making distinctions in typography.

f] One of the earliest of such designs is *Stone Informal* (1987) by Sumner Stone who is credited with first using the designation 'informal'.

1. Ullman (1960), pp 59–61.
2. Johnson (1959), pp 93, 94.
3. Johnson (1959), pp 103, 104.
4. Johnson (1959), p 109.
5. Carter (2002), p 124.
6. Johnson (1959), p 123.
7. Twyman (1993), p 109.
8. Willberg, Forssman (1997), pp 122–127.

Foreign words used in English are sometimes *italicized*, sometimes not, depending on how common they are. For instance, you would italicize your *bête noire* and your *Weltanschauung*, but not your croissant or your résumé.

Nevertheless, some writers — let's call them *overemphasizers* — just can't get enough *bold* and *italic*. If they feel strongly about the point they're making, they won't hesitate to run the whole paragraph in bold type. Don't be one of these people. This habit wears down your readers' retinas and their patience. It also gives you nowhere to go when you need to emphasize a word.

▲ *Avenir*, 1988, Linotype, with an oblique roman instead of italic.

❦LIB·I.

I n uillos abeunt uestes · in crura lacerti ·
F it lupus · et ueteris seruat uestigia formæ ·
C anicies eadem est · eadem uiolentia uultus ·
I idem oculi lucent · eadem feritatis imago est ·
O cidit una domus · sed non domus una perire
D igna fuit · qua terra patet · fera regnat Erinnýs ·
I n facinus iurasse putes · dent ocyus omnes ,
Q u as meruere pati(sic stat sententia)pœnas ·
D icta Iouis pars uoce probant · stimulos´q; frementi
A ddycyunt · alij partes assensibus implent ·
E st tamen humani generis iactura dolori
O mnibus · et · quæ sit terræ mortalibus orbæ
F orma futura · rogant · quis sit laturus in aras
T hura · feris ne paret populandas tradere terras ·
T alia quærentes(sibi enim fore cætera curæ)
R ex superum trepidare uetat · sobolem´q; priori
D issimilem populo promittit origine mira ·
I am´q; erat in totas sparsurus fulmina terras ·
S ed timuit · ne forte sacer tot ab ignibus æther
C onciperet flammas · totus´q; ardesceret axis ·
E sse quoq; in fatis reminiscitur affore tempus ·
Q uo mare , quo tellus , correpta´q; regia cœli
A rdeat · et mundi moles operosa laboret ·
T ela reponuntur manibus fabricata Cyclopum ·
P œna placet diuersa · genus mortale sub undis

croyez-vous connoître en plaisanterie, croyez-vous que le *pouvoir prochain* et la *grace suffisante* fussent des sujets plus divertissants que tout ce que vous appellez les visions de Desmarêts? Cependant vous ne nous persuaderez pas que les dernieres *imaginaires* soient aussi agréables que les premieres *provinciales;* tout le monde lisoit les unes, et vos meilleurs amis peuvent à peine lire les autres.

▲ The first italic type cut in 1501 by Francesco Griffo. Actual size.

▲ The italic of François-Ambroise Didot and Pierre-Louis Vafflard, c. 1783. Actual size.

In probability theory, two events are independent, statistically independent, or stochastically independent if the occurrence of one does not affect the probability of occurrence of the other.

When coding, our scripts need to communicate with each other, need references to items in the game and need to pass data around with efficiency and speed.

Please explore the updated edition.
Please explore the updated edition.
Please explore the updated edition.

⏛ *Galliard* italic, 1978, Linotype.　　▲ The three italics of *Auto*, 2014, Underware.

⏏ *Pique*, 2014, Process Type Foundry.

Dieſe »Zweite Probe einer neu verän=
derten Druckſchrift” iſt ein Sonderdruck von
Johann Friedrich Ungers Vorwort zu
dem Buche, in dem die jetzt gebräuchliche
»Unger=Fraktur” zum erſtenmal angewen=
det worden iſt:

◀ Johann Friedrich Unger, *Unger-Fraktur*,
1794: emphasis achieved by spacing
instead of italic.
From: *Zweite Probe neu veränderter Deutscher
Druckschrift*, 1794, J.F. Unger.

The greater the slope, the greater the distortion.

The way that people construe their practice is their informal theory. The challenge is to make this informal theory or personal construction of practice explicit.

▲ *Joanna* italic, 1930–1931, Monotype.   ▲ *Alverata* informal, 2013, TypeTogether.

17 Large and small: to be seen, to be read

When you are really wrapped up in a text, you often fail to notice the letters and accompanying signs – this is generally the fate of typefaces used for text set in small sizes.[a] Reading is then close to automatic, and words, sentences and their meaning seem to flow directly from page or screen into the brain.[1] Such a reading experience is aided by a generous dose of conventionality – when readers want to reach the content of a text as easily or quickly as possible, that is what they expect. They often have different expectations when reading large sizes, for example headlines; then the unexpected and unconventionality are presumably not expected but often accepted [see chapter 5].

a] This is what Beatrice Warde wrote about in her essay *The Crystal Goblet or Printing Should Be Invisible*. Warde (1956), pp 11–17.

Many type designs have been made to be used specifically in large sizes, such as the script *Mistral* (1953) designed by Roger Excoffon. Clearly this is not the typeface for a lengthy text set in a small type size, although it was cast by the Fonderie Olive in Marseille in 12 point as the smallest size.[b] *Mistral* is easy to read but was obviously designed principally to be seen. Where seeing stops and reading begins depends, of course, on the type design, the type size, and the length of a text, but, during immersed reading of a lengthy text set in a small size, seeing never entirely stops. And when you look at a few words set in a large type size you cannot help but read.

b] These are Didot-points, one of which measured a little less than 0.376 mm. It was slightly larger than the Anglo-American Pica-point. The present day DTP-point is defined as 1/72 of an inch or about 0.353 mm.

However, display faces, as a broad category, are made more to look at than to be read, and conversely text faces, as an equally broad category, are made more to be read than to be seen. There are no precise definitions of a display and text typefaces. Text faces are usually conventional, measured, and meant for sustained reading, while display faces are often outspoken, eccentric, can show fancy traits ostentatiously, and can be unconventional and even inconsistent, to some extent. This can affect their legibility and can render them unfit for text in small sizes.

Generally, display typefaces are intended for use at large sizes in short texts, while text faces are used mostly in small sizes for substantial amounts of text.

What are large and small sizes? In chapter 10 above, 18 point was mentioned as large and 10 point as a small size in relation to pattern and texture. Possibly 14 point, with a total height of a little more than 5 mm, is the smallest size wherein a display face can still grab the attention to full advantage. As explained before, it depends upon the x-height whether the letters are experienced as large or small; the x-height of 14 point *Mistral* (Didot points) is on average 1.7 mm, while the x-height of Excoffon's *Antique Olive* regular (1962–1966) at 14 point is 3 mm.

Many text faces still function satisfactorily way above 10 point; they will probably not make for exciting titles or headlines but will do the job anyway. This leaves a kind of grey area between 10 and 14 point, in which, for example, 12 point is large for a text face and too small for most display faces. German type designers and typographers have 'Lesegraden' and 'Schaugraden' – sizes for reading and those for looking at. The first range from 8 to 12 point and the latter from 14 point upwards.[2]

For quite some time already the distinctions between text and display faces have been blurred, with text faces acquiring details that attract the attention of readers in large sizes and make for a spirited looking text in small sizes, when details subside into a texture. This development has its origin in the nineteenth century, when Egyptians appeared around 1820 and were later developed into Ionics and Clarendons [see chapter 7] for both text and display.[3] Increasingly, type designers now try to reconcile the qualities of text and display faces so that a type design can be scaled up and down without unpleasant surprises for readers. This is easier to do with a sanserif than with a seriffed design because of its relative simplicity, and explains why sanserifs have been moving away from the rather neutral designs of the late 1950s, such as *Helvetica* and *Univers* (both 1957). In the years after their introduction these typefaces became increasingly accepted as text faces, while from the end of the twentieth century their neutrality began to be contested and more idiosyncratic sanserifs began to appear, such as *Gitan* (2016, originally designed as *Sherpa* in 2013) by Florian Runge (1986–). Instead of classifying this design as a sanserif, it can be seen as a typeface with rudimentary serifs.

c] Tobias Frere-Jones and Cyrus Highsmith have collaborated with Matthew Carter on this design. – https://en.wikipedia.org/wiki/Miller_(typeface) (12/10/2017).

d] Slimbach (1994), p 25. *Adobe Jenson* was published as a multiple master typeface.

Type designs are often adapted for use in large and small sizes, the version for the small sizes being a little wider, bolder and with wider inter-character spaces in comparison to the slightly condensed, lightened and more tightly fitted version for large sizes – as was done for *Miller* (1997) by Matthew Carter.[c] A practice from the hot-metal era was revived at Adobe by creating 'optical sizes' for *Adobe Jenson* (1994) with 6-, 12- and 72-point masters or primary fonts.[d]

1. See chapter 0, note 4.
2. Forssman (2002), p 63.
3. Gray (1954), pp 23–26, 66, 67.

The x-height of 14 point Mistral is on average 1.7 mm,
while the x-height of Antique Olive at 14 point is 3 mm.

All writing involves a planning stage.
All writing involves a planning stage.
All writing involves a planning stage.
All writing involves a planning stage.
All writing involves a planning stage.
All writing involves a planning stage.
All writing involves a planning stage.
All writing involves a planning stage.
All writing involves a planning stage.
All writing involves a planning stage.
All writing involves a planning stage.
All writing involves a planning stage.
All writing involves a planning stage.
All writing involves a planning stage.
All writing involves a planning stage.

▲ *Mistral*, 1953, and *Antique Olive*, 1962–1966, both 14 point.

▲ Many text faces still function satisfactorily way above 10 point. *Capitolium*, 1998, TypeTogether, from 24 to 10 point.

Even though the information seems rudimentary, a review of the basics now and then will ensure that you will respond appropriately in emergency situations.

A miller is a person who operates a mill, a machine to grind a cereal crop to make flour.

Milling is among the oldest of human occupations.

heavier serifs
& stems

wider charaters

looser letterfit

Hmfg

larger
x-height

open counterforms

6-POINT

Hmfg

12-POINT

Hmfg

72-POINT

A comparison between the regular 6,- 12-, and 72-point primary fonts scaled to the same H-height.

⬟ *Gitan*, 2016, Rosetta.

⬟ *Miller* for text (above) and display (below), 1997, Carter & Cone.

▲ Masters or primary fonts for *Jenson*, 1994, Adobe.
From: Robert Slimbach, *Adobe Jenson: a Contemporary Revival*, 1994, Adobe Systems Incorporated.

18 Typography

Writing is formulating and organizing thoughts and ideas, and capturing these in words and sentences to pass them on to readers. This is the domain of authors. To turn their work into typography, to make it accessible and attractive, is the domain of typographers and graphic designers, and of type designers as well. Typeface selection is often based on a textual genre: a popular impression is that subject plays a role, that a romantic novel requires a romantic looking typeface or a mathematical work an exact looking one. Only very rarely will a choice of typeface be so literal; usually choosing a font has a less specific reason and is linked to much wider categories of text or identities [see chapter 19], or to the general aim to read comfortably, independent of subject matter or even of genre or medium. And personal preferences naturally play a part in the choice of a typeface.

The creation of new kinds of type designs has occasionally led to new ways of dealing with typography, as with the wide variety of display faces developed during the nineteenth century, resulting in posters with nearly as many typefaces as lines of text on them.[1] And Adrian Frutiger's design of *Univers* (1957), a systematized type family, encouraged the emergence of tightly organized or 'programmed' typography, based on grids, which made many texts closely resemble one another.[2]

There is more to typography than organizing text or making the work of an author legible. Type is often combined and integrated with illustrations, colour, space, and the material qualities of an object like a book, magazine, or newspaper. To create striking and attractive designs has always been part of typography. Type design, typography, and graphic design have often been touched by movements in design and the arts in general [see chapters 20 and 25], as well as by developments in society.

Space has always been a part of typography – around text and images as margins, and to separate elements or group them together (for instance, to make clear that a caption accompanies a particular illustration). But from the late 1920s modernist typographers such as Jan Tschichold gave space a much more prominent role as an element in the composition of pages with asymmetrical arrangements of text and images.

Otherwise, type designs come alive in typography: it's like wearing clothes – on a hanger they may look nice, but only when worn do they show up well. The tasks posed by different genres of text have resulted in differing interpretations of typography (and of the role of typefaces in it): 'Typography may be defined as the craft of rightly disposing printing material in accordance with specific purpose; of so arranging the letters, distributing the space and controlling the type as to aid to the maximum the reader's comprehension of the text.'[3] This definition by Stanley Morison, with emphasis on maximum comprehension, clearly refers to long texts for deep reading and the conventional typefaces fit for that purpose [see chapters 5 and 6]. An alternative definition was given by Günther Gerhard Lange (1921–2008), who for many years led the type design department of Berthold, a German foundry, manufacturer of phototypesetting machines, and publisher of many good type designs: 'Typography is the staging of a message on a surface'.[a] With 'staging' this interpretation refers to the kinds of typography that appear in magazines and advertisements – special interests of Lange – with a lively handling of headline faces and texts in relation to pictures, which can differ from page to page.[b]

Printed matter used to be neatly divided into stable genres such as books, magazines, newspapers, annual reports, advertising and – in the heyday of 33rpm vinyl discs – record sleeves. To some extent this classification still exists, although the advent and development of the Internet and the worldwide web have significantly shaken it up: some genres, such as dictionaries, now mainly appear online, and others, like newspapers, books, and magazines, have parallel online versions; and there are new genres on the web such as blogs and tweets. Also, distinctions between newspapers, magazines, brochures, and some other categories of printed matter have been blurred and mixed on the web.

Several of the printed genres had their own typographic characteristics and typefaces. There is, for instance, the archetypal newspaper, illustrated magazine, or novel, each with their own distinct typography and types. The general category of newspaper typefaces have already been discussed [see chapter 7] and book faces are an equally general category. The bookiest of all bookish typefaces is probably *Bembo* (1929), a favourite of many book designers. In fashion magazines, descendants of the work of the Didots and Bodoni (letterforms with extremely thin horizontal parts) appear more often than in other genres, especially in titles and headlines. As newspapers are printed so well in the twenty-first century, their typical typefaces, such as *Excelsior* (1931), have faded away and many typefaces that could not function very well in newspapers before the introduction of computer-to-plate (CTP) in 1994 [see chapter 8] can now

a] This definition was passed on to me in 2011 by Erik Spiekermann, who was closely acquainted with Lange. In German it is: 'Typografie ist die Inszenierung einer Mitteilung in der Fläche.' A definition by Gerrit Noordzij is: 'Writing with prefabricated letters.' (Noordzij, 1988, p 12); and by Gavin Ambrose and Paul Harris: 'Typography is the means by which a written idea is given a visual form.' (Ambrose, 2005, p 6). Joseph Moxon has written in 1683: 'By a typographer, I do not mean a printer, as he is vulgarly accounted, ... But by a typographer, I mean such a one, who by his own judgement, from solid reasoning with himself, can either perform, or direct others to perform from the beginning to end, all the handy-works and physical operations relating to typographie.' (Moxon, 1978, pp 11, 12).

b] In 1985 I visited G.G. Lange at his home, where he was collecting sample pages from stacks of magazines to track trends in magazine typography.

be used. And telephone directories, with a highly specialized typeface like *Bell Centennial* (1978)[4] by Matthew Carter, have disappeared completely, though *Bell Centennial* is still used now and then because of its strong characteristics. *Bell Centennial* had to withstand fast printing with thin inks on rough and absorbent paper, and the resulting look is now appreciated as a spicy flavour.

Few technological limitations are left for type designers to meet, and instead of technology-based designs more and more genre-bound fonts are now being made, as atmosphere values have come to the fore [see chapter 19]: for example in magazines – about cars, sports, celebrity and entertainment, and many more subjects. But it is difficult for genre-specific designs to stay within their genres. Often such type designs are used in kinds of written communication for which they were not designed. This happened before, for instance with *Swift* (1985), which was designed for newspapers but has been used often in books or annual reports. Nonetheless, specific typefaces in printed genres still contribute to the typical visual programmes of such categories, while on the web typefaces do not indicate genres so clearly. Several decades into the twenty-first century, the possibility to recognize a textual genre on the web by its typeface is still weak. Especially in body texts, generic sanserifs appear often – a situation that may change. Actually, typefaces are a prominent means to stand out on the web.

In the 1960s the transition began from hot metal to digital typefaces, a process covering roughly three decades and happening in waves. During the first wave, metal type, hand- and machine-set, was replaced by phototypesetting, with early digital typesetting close behind. In the late 1980s Macintoshes ushered in the demise of many phototypesetting studios, foundries, and manufacturers of typesetting equipment. The production of hot-metal Linotype machines, for example, was already terminated in the USA in 1971 and in England in 1984.[5] In 1985 the Stempel Foundry in Frankfurt closed its doors and in 1993 Berthold, then manufacturer of internationally renowned phototypesetting equipment, went out of business. With each wave, many experienced typesetters, operators of typesetting machines, and other experts were laid off or retrained, and with them much typographic expertise evaporated. In the 1990s website designers turned to handling text, sometimes with scant knowledge of the intricacies of typography.

Despite the loss of knowledge, typography and type design survived quite well, partly because interested and knowledgeable authors handed down virtually all micro- and macro-typographic know-how to succeeding generations of typographers,[6] and because of the curiosity of next generations and the introduction of specialized courses for type design and typography in higher education. In this way the grammar of legibility [see chapter 3], the body of courtesies to readers, survived.

Type now acts on two distinctly different stages: on paper and on screen. An important characteristic of typography on paper is its usually tight organization, due to the costs of paper and printing. On the web this plays no role – the web has unlimited space. Behind, for example, the small frame of a mobile phone stretches endless digital space to be scrolled, swiped and clicked. As a consequence web typography can be quite loose or even disjointed.

From the start, around 1450, typography has been systematic, based on rectangular pieces of metal. Seen from above (with the characters mirrored on top), these metal blocks varied in height (type size) and width, and were assembled in larger rectangles, from pages of books to newspaper pages. When produced by typesetting machines, their height was measured in points (Didot and Pica) and their widths in units.[c] The metal bodies have disappeared, yet the character-containing rectangles remain, rooted beyond typography in the layouts of manuscripts.[7] Metal matrices and type bodies limited the lengths of overhanging parts of letters (or in some cases made these impossible, as with Linotype) but, in digital typography, overhanging parts no longer cause any problems. Typography is still systematic, with letters and other signs grouped into words and lines, which are then stacked as paragraphs or columns. Unjustified typesetting (with varying line lengths) is at least as common as justified typesetting, and the freedom to reshape blocks of text and to move them around on a surface has increased greatly with digital typography.

[c] For the development and introduction of the Didot and Pica points see: Boag (1996), pp 105–121. For the Monotype machine the widths of letters and other signs, sidebearings included, were based on 18 units. 'In the 1950s most if not all of Linotype's newspaper faces were adapted to the Teletypesetter (tts) system which was based on 18 units to the em. General purpose Linotype faces were not unitized. The first Linotype phototypesetting machine, the Linofilm, had an 18-unit spacing system. The Linofilm's successor, the V-I-P, had a 54-unit system.' Matthew Carter in an email (28/09/2017).

1. Gray (1976), pp 135–145.
2. Gerstner (1968), *passim*.
3. Morison (1930), p 61.
4. Re (2002), pp 20–23, 57, 58.
5. https://de.wikipedia.org/wiki/ Linotype-Setzmaschine (11/04/2017).
6. See chapter 3, note c.
7. Gumbert (1993), pp 5–28.

▶ A poster with a variety of display faces, 1841, 66.2 × 52.2 cm.
COLLECTION OF MICHAEL TWYMAN

MEN OF LINDSEY!

LOOK TO LINCOLN!

NOBLY have the **FARMERS** responded to the **FREEMEN's** call. **Bulwer** has paid the forfeit of his **Treachery,** and is driven from our **County!**

ANOTHER

VICTORY

Awaits **your** Exertions, and you are saved. Rest not till you have deprived that Government, who are determined on your ruin, of ANOTHER of their **strongest supporters---LORD WORSLEY,** by **rejecting him** also on the day of Election, and

VOTE FOR

Christopher & Cust,

The steady Opponents of your Enemies,

The former of whom will lead you to Victory under the Banners of ORANGE-and-PURPLE, and the latter under those of PINK.

LOUTH, June 30, 1841.

William Edwards, Printer, in the Corn-Market, Louth.

Karl Gerstner:

Programme entwerfen

Programm als Formlehre
Programm als Denklehre
Programm als Raster
Programm als Photographie
Programm als Literatur
Programm als Musik

Programm als Schrift
Programm als Typographie
Programm als Bild
Programm als Methode

Verlag Arthur Niggli AG

VOGUE

Meanwhile, a behind-the-scenes battle of the sexes rages, as the Washington Post balances the demands of its investors with the awful truth that "the only way to protect the right to publish is to publish!"

ABCDEFGHIJKLMNOPQRSTUVWXYZ&
abcdefghijklmnopqrstuvwxyz 1234567890
ABCDEFGHIJKLMNOPQRSTUVWXYZ&
abcdefghijklmnopqrstuvwxyz 1234567890
ABCDEFGHIJKLMNOPQRSTUVWXYZ&
abcdefghijklmnopqrstuvwxyz 1234567890
ABCcDEFGHIJKLMNOPQRSTUVWXYZ&

⬔ The masthead of *Vogue* magazine.

⬔ *Excelsior*, 1931, Linotype.

◀ Karl Gerstner, *Programme entwerfen*, 1968, Arthur Niggli, 25.4 × 18.5 cm.

▲ *Bell Centennial* address, sub-caption, name and number, bold listing, 1978. AT&T for the telephone directories in the USA. Enlarged
From: Matthew Carter, *A Check-list of Typefaces Designed by Matthew Carter*, 2002, Carter & Cone.

▲ The character-containing rectangles remain.

19 Expression

Expressivity has become one of the main incentives for the creation of new typefaces by the younger generations of designers, as personal interpretations, or as a voice for the time they live in and for what is happening around them. As digitization has freed type design of many restrictions, for instance high production costs or being tied to typesetting machines (such as Monotype and Linotype), and with the increasing influence of the web, type design has become more and more a tool for marketing. This has stimulated the interest in semantics (purely graphic not linguistic) – the connotations of typefaces or their power of expression.

This aspect of type design is known by several descriptions, such as 'the relationship between content and form',[1] 'atmosphere value',[2] 'congeniality',[3] 'rhetoric' – using graphic expression persuasively – 'type and emotion',[4] and 'type and personality' – the personality of the typeface, not of the designer – and also as 'font psychology'.[5] Research on this subject, the correspondence between the personality of a typeface – what it represents – and the susceptibility of readers to this, began in 1920, ran through the 1930s,[6] and culminated in a study by G.W. Ovink (1912–1984) in 1938.[7] Since then many publications have followed without fundamental new insights emerging.

Typefaces can have a person- or group-identifying capability.[8] They can identify many kinds of products, brands, institutions, businesses or individuals. Typical typographic genres or categories of printed products that use typefaces for profiling are newspapers and magazines. This is a process that works by association and through habituation; the choice of a typeface to identify, say, a brand, can lead to it being identified with that brand. If the combination of a specific typeface with a product or a brand is presented to the public often enough, so that readers are sufficiently massaged mentally, the process can work. This can be a precarious process though, as letterforms are abstract shapes and it is none too easy to provide them with readily interpretable characteristics which clearly correspond to the properties of what they have to represent.

Linguists call the intended effect of an utterance (in this case a typographic one) its 'illocutionary force', and how it affects its audience (in this case its readership) as the 'perlocutionary effect'.[9] This terminology can be used by type designers, typographers, website and graphic designers as well.

A famous example of the identification of a kind of typeface with a category of printed matter, newspapers, is Imperial (1954), a typical newspaper typeface designed by Edwin Shaar (1915–2001) for the Intertype Corporation.[a] *Imperial* was designed, like other newspaper typefaces, to withstand the effects of stereotyping, rough paper, thin ink, and high press-speeds. Such typefaces became so closely associated with newspapers that they were hardly ever used in other genres of print.

The closest associations of letterforms and subjects can be found in logotypes – brand names or signs – such as the Coca-Cola logo (1885), designed by the firm's bookkeeper F.M. Robinson (1845–1923),[10] or that of St Raphaël (1948), a French aperitif, designed by Charles Loupot (1892–1962). In such cases legibility is not of overriding importance; habituation or familiarization can lead to a trade mark being recognized immediately without reading being involved.

An example of a type design successfully associated with a city, London, and its public transport is the Underground typeface (1916) designed by Edward Johnston; and another successful match was made between a set of letters and a supranational political entity: the Roman Imperial capitals representing the Roman Empire, an association that still functions long after the empire has disappeared. A divorced association is the one between the newspaper *The Times* and *Times New Roman* (1931); one year after its introduction in the paper the typeface was released for commercial sale and became famous in its own right. From the late 1950s *Helvetica* (1957) was internationally adopted as a corporate typeface, not representing a single firm or institution but all those who wanted to look up-to-date and modern, a recurring phenomenon in graphic design and typography.

Contrary to the possibility of designing an expressive typeface is the wish to make a neutral design for the widest attainable application. Several sanserifs come close to this ideal, such as *Source Sans Pro* (2012) designed by Paul D. Hunt (1977–) for Adobe.[b] Often type designs endowed with a particular connotation will lose their original meaning over time and can acquire a new identity, or end up being neutral. This happened to *Helvetica* and *Univers* (both 1957), once models of modernity signifying progress, and now modern classics without a precisely determinable atmosphere value.

While the association of a few letters or a complete type design with a product, an organization, or a genre of publication can be successful, evaluations of the connotations of letterforms can be vague, especially when the semantic differential is applied.[11] This tool functions with ratings on scales between

a] In 2007 *The New York Times* changed to a narrower page and Matthew Carter was asked to improve the copyfitting of *Imperial* (more characters to a line) to make up for the loss from the new page width. 'I found the *Imperial* characters were still on their 18-unit Teletypesetter set-widths. I edited the fonts to make them fit better, and removed some of the remnants of slug-machine constraints. In the course of doing this the face departed slightly from the original Intertype version.' (Matthew Carter in an e-mail of 26/02/2017.) *Imperial* is still used by the *The New York Times*.

b] *Source Sans Pro* was partly inspired by sanserifs designed by Morris Fuller Benton (or in the design of which Morris Fuller Benton was involved) for American Type Founders in the early part of the twentieth century. It is combined with similarly neutral versions of the Chinese, Japanese and Korean scripts.

opposing notions, such as feminine and masculine, expensive and cheap, passive and active, cool and warm, and so on. When subjects are asked to associate freely and to associate type designs with adjectives to describe connotations or atmosphere values, only rarely do the criteria of the semantic differential come up; mostly more general notions emerge, such as 'warm', 'spiky', or 'corporate'. And when type designers are asked to meet specific needs, such as: 'distinctive – characterful letterforms that show a unique personality; simple – accessible and easy to read across all media; sympathetic – rounded characters with a soft and human feel', then several type designs can answer such requirements.[c]

c] Quoted from a recent (confidential) briefing from a marketing agency.

This topic brings together the rational approach to type design and the emotional perspective. Type design, being indirect, requires planning, sketching out early ideas, turning these into test fonts, planning a range, and more – a rational process [see chapter 2]. Type designers have for a long time combined such an approach with ideas about how to touch readers. When Nicolas Jenson started using gothic type in 1473/4 for legal and religious texts he did so because readers engaged in law and theology were accustomed to these letterforms, just as humanists wanted to read printed texts with letterforms they favoured, based on their handwriting. (This is only surprising as we now tend to see his classic roman as more progressive than gothic letterforms.) Jenson also needed gothic type because his competitor in Venice, Wendelin von Speyer, was printing books with such letterforms from 1472.[12]

These are decisions based on rational considerations, but the sensitivities of readers definitely had a share in them. It is not a question of one or the other, of either rationalism or responding to readers' feelings. It can be argued that all type designs ever made reflect both aspects in different proportions. As habituation is such a strong influence on legibility, any deviation from those forms to which readers are accustomed will cause an emotional response, and if people can read letterforms they like to see and are familiar with, no matter how rational the letterforms or the readers may be, then they are reassured, which is an emotional response too. Obviously, equipping letterforms with specific expressive features to entice readers goes much further than gently responding to readers' expectations, but both strategies are of an emotional or psychological nature.

Letters can be finished to look handmade, worn, or tatty. In most type designs the contours have been carefully smoothed and freed of bumps or dimples. In metal type, it was especially in the category of script typefaces that all kinds of effects were applied to simulate the use of brushes, chalk, or other writing instruments on a rough surface.[13] The letters of a well-considered design like *Mistral* (1953) by Roger Excoffon were softened by taking a kind of small bites out of the contours.[14] With digitization such effects can be applied much more easily than to metal letters, and consequently the number of fake handmade and worn letters has increased enormously. In the end, these are mostly simple cliches to create an atmosphere of cosiness and confidentiality. Although such letters have an air of informality, they are thoroughly formal in being repeatable in the conventional way, unless many alternative glyphs are provided.

1. Spencer (1968), pp 29, 30.
2. Ovink (1938), pp 127–177.
3. Zachrisson (1965), pp 73–84.
4. Many websites, for example (all consulted on 06/02/2017): https://www.atypi.org/conferences/barcelona-2014/programme/activity?a=425; http://www.companyfolders.com/blog/font-psychology-how-typefaces-hack-our-brains; https://blog.hubspot.com/marketing/typography-emotions#sm.0000uke5dbudyfr6vth1cmfne8h8o; https://www.microsoft.com/typography/links/News.aspx?NID=6412; http://usabilitynews.org/the-effect-of-typeface-on-the-perception-of-email/.
5. https://www.templatemonster.com/blog/font-psychology/ (06/02/2017).
6. Spencer (1968), p 29.
7. Ovink (1938), pp 127–177.
8. Crystal (1998), pp 7–23.
9. Crystal (1998), p 13.
10. https://en.wikipedia.org/wiki/Coca-Cola#Logo_design (09/02/2017).
11. Dyson (2016), pp 227–245.
12. Lowry (1991), p 96.
13. Jaspert (1970), pp 361–405.
14. Gineste (2010), pp 148–171.

ABC NOP
DEF QRS
GHIJTUW
KLM XYZ

▲ Roman Imperial capitals that the author, as
a student, copied in 1963.

Once upon a time newspapers were the primary source of national and local news and created the record of our lives; Births, marriages, deaths, accidents, arrests, photographs, family reunions – everything was in the newspaper. Now those old newspapers are an irreplaceable source for hundreds of years of history featuring the most notable historical events like the Civil War, World War 1, World War 2, the Vietnam War, Pearl Harbor, the Great Depression, and more.

◀ *Imperial*, 1954, Intertype.

▼ The St Raphaël logo with guidelines for wall painters.
From: *Charles Loupot*, 1979, Musée de l'Affiche.

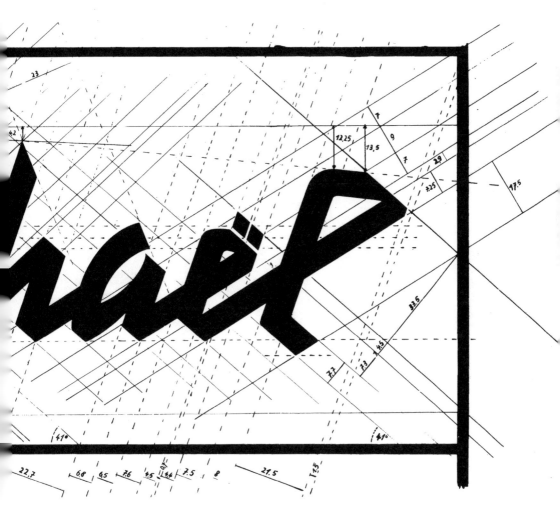

By staying neutral, I end up being somebody that everybody can trust. **Even if they don't always agree with my decisions, they know I'm not working against them.**

▲ *Source Sans Pro*, 2012, Adobe.

▲ *Mistral*, 1953, softened by small bites taken out of the contours of the letters.

20 Time, place, personality

Type designs can show when, where, and by whom they are made. Timelessness does not exist. Although the letterforms of Claude Garamond are over four-and-half centuries old and are still in use, the original shapes are firmly rooted in the French Renaissance, while all designs copied from or inspired by these differ considerably from the original and are clearly from the twentieth century. What happens often, though, is that typefaces exceed their life expectancy or the life of their makers, while other designs have a limited life. One of the latter is *Reiner Script* (1951) designed by Imre Reiner (1900–1987), undeniably belonging to the 1950s, a period between primary Modernism and its extension after World War II, which is partly characterized by a short-lived interest in whimsical shapes[1] as a response to the square, circle and triangle of the previous movement.[a]

All type designs are products of the time they were made and used in, affected by the lives of their designers, whose minds are formed by multiple experiences – by education, general and professional, or, for instance, by colleagues with whom they have an affinity or work together. Type designs are, like other products of the human mind and hands, influenced by what goes on in society and by cultural experiences, by art seen, books read, or music heard. As letters and other typographic signs are such abstract shapes, the traces of personality, place, and especially time are not always easy to detect and to interpret. This side of type design is part of its history and also of art history, divided into periods that must be studied to be distinguished, recognized, and understood.

In the 1920s and 1930s sanserifs were for some designers an instrument of a socialist worldview, representing equality, often by doing away with capitals. Not only should letterforms with serifs and Fraktur – then still used on a large scale in the German speaking part of the world – be abolished, but also scripts such as Greek, Cyrillic, and even Japanese and Chinese, which were thought to be nationalistic.[2] The more neutral a sanserif was, the better: and geometry was seen as the objective and unbiased basis for letterforms. This approach to type design went together with criticism of 'the old typography (1450–1914)'

a] The circle, square and triangle – along with the primary colors, blue, red and yellow – symbolize the Bauhaus (1919–1933), the famous school for designers and artists. The cover of the catalogue for the Bauhaus exhibition in the Stedelijk Museum, Amsterdam, in 1969, shows only these shapes and colours without any text.

and attention for 'the new art', with Cubism, Constructivism, Futurism and other movements as the foundation for 'the new typography'.[3]

In type design, criticism of previous designs and designers can be expressed.[4] When Eric Gill wrote his oft-quoted words: 'Letters are things, not pictures of things',[5] he was thinking of abundantly decorated, Victorian architectural lettering and other letterforms of the 'neo' styles then in fashion, such as neo-gothic. In response, Gill made significantly simpler and more sober letterforms.

The course of time brings about change, not only in the connotations of letterforms [see chapter 19] but also in preferences for letterforms among designers and users. From the late 1950s a new generation of sanserifs, such as *Univers* (1957), transmitted a connotation of modernity and progress, very much part of the post-war rebuilt world. This was a meaning these sanserifs lost in the 1970s. During the last decade of the twentieth century, *Helvetica* (1956) was shunned for being overused, yet early in the twenty-first century it returned quietly as a modern classic.[6] *Helvetica* has even been accused of domination, although during its heyday many other typefaces remained in use. Never in the history of typography and type design has one typeface or one kind of typeface dominated completely – as far as the Latin script is concerned.

How much are designers aware of the results of their work being caught in a restricted period or possibly having an extended life? How much do designers want their designs to have an abundant but short-lived success, or to keep going for a longer time? The closer you stay to the core of the 'typographic stellar cloud' [see chapter 6], the longer your design can last. And for text faces a longish existence can be expected anyway, while display faces often live brightly and briefly in the here and now.

Of course trends and fashion[b] or style have parts to play, as well as longer-term influences such as an engagement with or an understanding of society. That is what informed the work of many graphic and typographic designers in the 1920s and 1930s with an international orientation. Designers and artists of that period shared many ideas, from Moscow to Paris,[7] and from Italy and Switzerland to the Netherlands.[8]

b] Fashion usually means clothes. In the context of this theory it means: the prevailing or popular style, or the latest and most admired style. *Helvetica* and *Univers* were originally, in the late 1950s and early 1960s, used on the basis of principles about clear communication and combined with programmatic typography. After a number of years, during the 1960s they became the fashion.

As a part of style, fashion or a trend, novelty is a vital ingredient, but its value can fade quickly and may cause a type design to have a short active life. However, to create a typeface which is widely perceived as new, surprising and exciting, the letterforms do not need to differ enormously from predecessors. It is instructive to compare *Helvetica* (1957), greeted on appearance as a brand new, original and refreshing design, with a predecessor like *Akzidenz Grotesk* (1898).[9] Small changes in type design can be perceived by those who choose typefaces and those who read them as considerable differences.

The traffic in written communication on screen, with its fast pace and global reach, has brought about fundamental changes. Styles, trends and fashions are now disseminated much faster than was possible on paper. Any influence a place of origin could have on a type design has become unhinged by the Internet as international and intercontinental connections have increased.

Early in the twenty-first century it was still possible to distinguish, for example, a typical Dutch approach to type design, mostly practical and not too fancy; until the 1980s Dutch type designers were mainly engaged in the design of text faces.[10] Since then type design has received a growing international interest. For example, from the late 1980s it has become popular in South America – in Chile, Mexico, Argentina, and other countries – while it is difficult to point out any features that are specifically South-American.[11] Meanwhile Latin typefaces are not alone any longer but are designed together with other scripts such as Arabic, Thai, or Chinese; and they are no longer made only by users of the Latin script, but also by Indian, Armenian, or Korean designers.

A designer's personal interests and preferences unavoidably play a role in designing type, but are sometimes hard to detect. In the case of Imre Reiner, for instance, this is not difficult as most of his designs have a background in handwriting and are closely related to his lettering and graphic art, as well as to what many other graphic artists were doing during the same period.[12] In contrast to Reiner, the interests of Morris Fuller Benton seem harder to fathom. His output is large and diverse, with a script typeface like *Typo Upright* (1905) as well as historical revivals such as *Bodoni* (1909) and *Garamond* (1917). *Franklin Gothic* (1902) and *News Gothic* (1908), both attributed to him, have survived several waves of competing sanserifs, are still in use and remain examples and touchstones for present-day and upcoming designers. A reason for this diversity, and the consequent difficulty in discerning Benton's personal 'signature', is that he was not trained as a designer but as a mechanical engineer, and that his approach to type design was in large part due to two other persons.

The first was the general manager of the American Type Founders Company, Robert W. Nelson (1851–1926). As ATF lost the market for small type-sizes to typesetting machine manufacturers, and had to compete with these, Nelson saw that for foundry type 'the future of the type industry depended on a never-ceasing succession of new typefaces of a new order of type design, now known as publicity type – type which is adapted as well as for text pages as for display pages'.[13] This became the firm's policy and Benton implemented it. The other person who contributed to Benton's prolific output was Henry Lewis Bullen (1857–1938), founder of ATF's Typographic Library in 1908 and its librarian until 1934. He provided Benton with ample historical material, including incunabula, for several of his revivals.[14] In cooperation with these men, Morris Fuller Benton worked more as an art director than as a type designer.[c]

The words of Nelson are, by the way, applicable to the design and use of type in the early part of the twenty-first century. Many recently designed typefaces are meant to strike the eyes in large sizes and to offer a pleasant and smooth reading experience in small sizes.

c] In the APA-Journal of June 2013 Rick von Holdt questions Morris Fuller Benton's reputation as one of the most prolific type designers ever. Von Holdt's assertion is that most of the work on ATF's type designs has been done by staff of the drawing office and several freelance designers. '[T]he reason he has been given credit as the "designer" is due to the fact that his name is listed on all of ATF's patent applications for those faces.' (Von Holdt (2013), p 11.) Benton headed ATF's type design department from 1900 to 1937. Which faces he designed himself or made a considerable personal contribution to is now very difficult, if not impossible, to ascertain. To assume that he functioned more as an art director than a type designer seems to be the best solution. – https://apa-letterpress.com/?m= 201306 (29/04/2017)

1. Burchartz (1953), p 43.
2. Tschichold (1928), p 77.
3. Tschichold (1928), pp 15–65.
4. Kinross (1997), pp 77–87.
5. Gill (1940), p 120.
6. Müller (2008), *passim*.
7. Hulten (1979), *passim*.
8. Spencer (1969), *passim*.
9. https://de.wikipedia.org/wiki/Akzidenz-Grotesk (19/03/2017).
10. Middendorp (2004), *passim*.
11. Kudrnovská (2015), p 75.
12. Turner Berry (1962), p 413.
13. Cost (2011), p 104.
14. Cost (2011), pp 104–107, 213.

Expressief

▲ *Reiner Script*, 1951, Lettergieterij Amsterdam.

▼ Different scripts seen as promoting nationalism.
From: Jan Tschichold, *Die neue Typographie*, 1928, Verlag des Bildungsverbandes der Deutschen Buchdrucker.

Fraktur

Schwabacher   Gotisch

Griechisch

Cyrillisch
(= Russisch und Bulgarisch)

Türkisch (= Arabisch)

Chinesisch (= Japanisch)

Indisch

Schriften der Exoten
(Zulukaffern, Papuas usw.)

= NATIONALISMUS

Small changes
Small changes

Akzidenz Grotesk   Helvetica

Considerable differences
Considerable differences

▲ Comparison of *Akzidenz Grotesk*, 1898, and *Helvetica*, 1957.

▲ The symbols of the Bauhaus, circle, triangle and square, turned into whimsical shapes.
From: Max Burchartz, *Gestaltungslehre*, 1953, Prestel Verlag.

▶ Letterforms from the end of the thirteenth century as an example for nineteenth-century lettering. Reduced.
From: Henry Shaw, *The Handbook of Mediaeval Alphabets*, 1853, Bernard Quaritch.

166

A A B C D O
E F G H I K L
M N O P Q
R S T T U V
W X Y Z Z
HIC · EST
MEN

60 Point   3 A 9 a

Distinguished

48 Point   3 A 10 a

Acknowledgment

◀ *Typo Upright*, 1905,
American Type Founders.

72 Point   3 A 4 a

Elks

72 Point   3 A 4 a

Right

48 Point   3 A 6 a

Rejoin

48 Point   4 A 8 a

Intrepid

24 Point   5 A 11 a

QUARTZ
Borough

24 Point   7 A 14 a

REPRODUCED
Neat Pamphlet

18 Point   8 A 17 a

NITROGEN
Hymnology

18 Point   11 A 22 a

MENAGERIE
Big elephant

12 Point   14 A 29 a

QUICK SERVICE
Important Notes

12 Point   17 A 34 a

RECEIVED NICELY
Brilliant statesman

▲ *Franklin Gothic*, 1902, left, and *News Gothic*,
1908, right, American Type Founders.
From: *The Specimen Book and Catalogue*, 1923,
American Type Founders.

21 Legibility

Reading is the conversion of written or typeset text into linguistic meaning. This process has a sensory and neuronal part – the decoding of visual signs; and a cognitive part – the acquisition of meaning. Readers often have multiple experiences at the cognitive level: following and understanding a story or an argument, appreciating the author's prose style, or being irritated by the use of difficult-to-understand trade terms. Also, readers may notice features of macro-typography but rarely the typeface itself – although they are doubtless more aware of typefaces in the era of personal digital devices equipped with a font menu. In connection with the sensory and neuronal part, legibility can be defined as: the ease with which visual symbols can be decoded [see chapter 6].[1] Apart from the history of letterforms, legibility is probably the aspect of type design which has been studied and written about most. While legibility has been mentioned several times in previous chapters, here the question is how type design can benefit from a more focused interest in legibility.

Why and how someone reads are significant considerations. Sustained, deep or immersive reading have also been mentioned earlier, in connection with substantial quantities of text: for example, professional information for scientists, or literature for enlightenment or recreation. This form of reading is also referred to as fluent or extended reading, and linear reading. However, reading is never entirely linear or continuous but is often interrupted by pondering or going back; reading can be hampered by the complexity of a text and will speed up when the content grips, and so on. There is informative reading, as for study, which can involve several texts and several media simultaneously; consultative reading, as with a dictionary, or when selecting only parts of a text; even leafing through a book is a way of reading. Interactive reading is yet another way to deal with text – for example, by making notes and summaries, to engage in a kind of editing to increase comprehension.[2]

Apart from the intentions of readers, typography can invite you to settle down with a book. Several layers of information can be brought to the reader's attention by differentiating typography: there is activating typography as in advertisements, and staged typography as in children's books.[3] Various kinds of typography and different ways of reading can all have a bearing upon the choice and design of typefaces, although it is possible to design an all-rounder which may not be able to take on all of these tasks but certainly can handle the majority of them. Such an all-rounder may not be the most exciting typeface –

it will be most certainly a conventional design. Many such typefaces are doing an excellent job, such as *Minion* (1992) by Robert Slimbach.

The group behaviour of letters and other typographic signs [see chapter 9] plays a dominant role in reading, especially with regard to sustained or deep reading. A regular flow of text helps readers to proceed steadily and easily through a text and to build up an understanding of its content. In this context, the 'group' of group behaviour could be construed as being synonymous with 'word'. However, we do not read word by word but often pick up combinations of parts of words, and the letters of such groups are recognized nearly simultaneously.[4]

The kind of typefaces which up to the mid-1980s were almost exclusively used in the graphic industry and in publishing, and were intended for printing only (hence the label 'printing type'), are now widely used by many people in word processing on all kinds of devices, big and immobile, small and mobile. Typographic characters, formal letterforms, that enjoyed a shielded life within the graphic industry for centuries, are now used extensively for many kinds of digital communication, for mass writing by workaday writers in healthcare, by civil servants, and countless others with office jobs. Writing, as keyboarding on all digital devices, has increased substantially for many as a daily activity.[5] Writing by means of a keyboard has not replaced handwriting but is practised next to it on a large scale. Typographic characters appear in all digital communication on screens, even in the simplest tweet.

With this development written language has become more informal, employing colloquialisms, contractions, abbreviations, slang, and emoticons. These are major social changes with consequences for education, legibility and the research thereof. Type is now an important tool for social networking and its conventionality is an essential aid to get messages across to large groups of readers and to be understood easily. However, this does not make it mandatory for type designers to stick to the centre of convention [see chapter 6]. Individuality and informality continue to play a role in the design and choice of typefaces and will be appreciated by recipients of personal messages. In addition to these developments, lettering – forming texts manually by writing and drawing letterforms – is increasingly practised for many kinds of applications [see chapter 2].

With type having left its old territory to become more of an everyday object than ever before, choosing a typeface has become a more widespread activity. It used to be printers, publishers, typographers, and graphic designers who chose fonts, and who together were like a filter between authors and publishers on the one hand and readers on the other. Now every reader-writer, all users of digital devices can consider and choose fonts. Just as digitization caused the number of type designers to grow [see chapter 2], so it has increased the number of type users. This has not been followed by a big shift in type design or in preferences for typefaces. Probably users, without the knowledge available to designers, are well aware of the requirements for fonts, due to their reading experience.

Readers will not, or only very rarely, avoid an unconventional type design on principle; type designers rightly experiment and speculate with formality [see chapter 8] and convention, and count on the curiosity of many who choose fonts or read them. Obviously it is possible for someone to stop reading if the typeface is experienced as too uncommon or does not meet reading habits sufficiently. Convention, which coincides with familiarity, depends to a great extent on habituation; readers of newspapers tend not to like it when their daily text face is changed, and many then protest. These readers grow accustomed to the replacement which will quickly lose its novel appearance, and when ten years later the paper changes its layout and text face again – not a rare course of events in the newspaper world – the readers will protest again.

However, many such insights are hardly applicable to reading texts on the web, from screens. The choice of typefaces for the web differs from that for paper. From the late 1980s the use of sanserifs on screen has steadily increased and is now the dominant kind of typeface on the web. Low resolutions had much to do with this development, as serifs often could not be reproduced satisfactorily and became unclear and distracting elements. Although it has long been maintained that sanserifs are less legible than letters with serifs, no conclusive evidence has ever been found.[6] And, while serifs can now be reproduced adequately on screen thanks to high resolutions, sanserifs continue to be applied and read on screen on a wide basis, and are here to stay. Habituation evidently drives typographers, website and graphic designers towards choosing seriffed fonts when dealing with long texts to be printed on paper and towards sanserifs for the web.

Arial (1982)[a] is one of the much-used typefaces on the web and as a consequence also on printouts; yet, according to some research findings it is ill-suited for children learning to read, for instance.[b] This makes clear how influential the role of habituation is in the choice of typefaces and reading. *Arial* may be less legible than many other designs, partly because of small openings in **a**, **e**, **g** and **s**, but this hardly seems to affect the acceptance of *Arial* as a default typeface or as a self-selected font for many users – it is certainly not illegible and must be somewhere near the centre of the type cloud [see chapter 6] because of its frequent use.

a] *Arial* was designed by a team of ten people led by Robin Nicholas and Patricia Saunders for Monotype Typography.

b] Bessemans (2012). In Ann Bessemans' dissertation this was the first of her theses.

In connection with legibility a question for type designers is: can it be improved, and how? Many type designs are variations of historical models or on well known themes [see chapter 7], continuing and maintaining an existing and acceptable level of legibility. Many type designs are based on personal ideas, on individual wishes to leave a mark on letterforms, or they follow the current taste or fashion, the latest and popular style. Typefaces are designed for specific purposes, for a particular kind of publication or content, to fit an identity or to be economical, but legibility is usually retained at best and not improved.

Any hope for the acceptance of a completely new set of signs, such as *Shavian* (1960) designed by Ronald Kingsley Read (1887–1975), is unrealistic; habituation and convention as undercurrents are too strong to make a drastic change of script likely.[c] Besides, *Shavian* was developed in compliance with the wishes of George Bernard Shaw (1856–1950) for a simplified spelling of the English language and not to improve legibility. If legibility can be changed for the better then it is with small and barely perceptible steps.

c] Spencer (1968), pp 57–81. It needed a powerful politician, Mustafa Kemal Ataturk (1881–1938), to replace the Arabic script with the Latin script in Turkey in 1928.

Although type designers have so far received very few clues for enhancing legibility, some studies have yielded information on which improvements can be based.[d] Type designers should not wait any longer for research results to come their way, but formulate their questions and wishes, and study these together with scientists. Since digital type design was introduced in the mid-1980s, the many experimental designs made by students or professionals only rarely go beyond experimentation for its own sake. What is needed is the careful development of experimental variations of letterforms with speculative features that can be compared scientifically with each other as well as with existing designs. A collaboration between scientists and designers can make this possible, with scientific researchers contributing their investigative methodology and designers their understanding of the flexibility of letterforms and the adaptability of readers.[e]

d] Fiset (2008), pp 1161–1168; Beier (2013), pp 75–94. In both cases emphasizing endings of letters, such as tops of ascenders, has been found to be an improvement.

Many questions remain to be researched, such as: what do readers really notice of the details in a type design at small sizes, when the typographic signs dissolve into a texture? Why are sanserifs so persistent in typography on screen? What if we include the serifs once more in this research – in all the places where they normally occur, or only at the extremeties of letters? Over the past half century, x-heights have steadily been raised at the expense of ascenders and descenders; is this a good development for readers, would they read better if ascenders were lengthened again? And what about descenders? Another development is that slightly condensed letterforms, combined with

e] Most designers are not sufficiently familiar with scientific research while the majority of legibility studies are carried out by scientists who sometimes lack sufficient typographic knowledge for research that really is of interest to type designers. Meanwhile some type designers have developed a genuine interest in scientific methods and are working together with those scientific researchers who are familiar with type design and typography. See: Beier (2012), *passim*; Beier (2016) – http://visiblelanguage-journal.com/issue/202/article/1372 (04/03/2017); Reynolds (2017), p 34.

f] Bessemans (2012), p 318. These questions require further investigation, but clear answers seem probable.

the tendency towards equal width, have become common. What reads better below 12 point: letters of varied or more equal width; wide or narrow letterforms?[f]

Very different conditions for legibility than those for reading with a tablet or book in hand apply to signage. Reading distances are much longer and differ greatly, readers move, indoor and outdoor conditions diverge, or dimensions of signs require economical solutions for typography. Typefaces for signs are often given extra space in comparison with text faces, and are generally heavier than regular (more like semi-bold). Letters on signs may be reflective or backlit; light on a dark background or the reverse; and there are more conditions like these that are typical of signage. While much research has already been done in this field, the proposed collaboration between designers and scientists in legibility research may yet bring improvements in this area, too.

1. Bessemans (2012), pp 91–94. For the meanings of legibility and readability, see chapter 3, note a.
2. https://www.researchgate.net/publication/262337178_Is_Making_Written_Syntheses_an_Aid_to_the_Comprehension_of_Documentary_Sources (18/06/2017).
3. Willberg (1997), pp 14–65.
4. Larson (2004), pp 74–77.
5. Brandt (2015), pp 3–5.
6. See chapter 5, note h.

▶ *Shavian*, 1960.
From: H. Spencer, *The Visible Word*, 1968, Lund
Humphries.

LAVINIA [*composedly*] Yes, Captain: they love even
their enemies.

THE CAPTAIN. Is that easy?

LAVINIA. Very easy, Captain, when their enemies
are as handsome as you.

THE CAPTAIN. Lavinia: you are laughing at me.

LAVINIA. At you, Captain! Impossible.

THE CAPTAIN. Then you are flirting with me,
which is worse. Dont be foolish.

LAVINIA. But such a very handsome captain.

THE CAPTAIN. Incorrigible! [*Urgently*] Listen to
me. The men in that audience tomorrow will be
the vilest of voluptuaries: men in whom the only
passion excited by a beautiful woman is a lust to
see her tortured and torn shrieking limb from
limb. It is a crime to gratify that passion. It is
offering yourself for violation by the whole rabble
of the streets and the riff-raff of the court at the
same time. Why will you not choose rather a
kindly love and an honorable alliance?

LAVINIA. They cannot violate my soul. I alone can
do that by sacrificing to false gods.

THE CAPTAIN. Sacrifice then to the true God.
What does his name matter? We call him Jupiter.
The Greeks call him Zeus. Call him what you
will as you drop the incense on the altar flame;
He will understand.

LAVINIA. No. I couldnt. That is the strange thing,
Captain, that a little pinch of incense should

When it comes to writing a resume, there a
few rules everyone is familiar with — avoid
typos, and don't lie. But many applicants skip
over crucial opportunities to show attention
to detail, like choosing the perfect font.

Font choice is another way to present yourself to the recruiter and hiring manager. And
research shows that font influences how
readers perceive a message.

A poorly selected font can indeed derail
one's chances for an interview, especially if
other factors aren't as strong.

▶ *Minion*, 1992, Adobe.

Amsterdam
Bergen
Castelré
Drouwenermond
Eck en Wiel
Foxhol
Gauw
Hantumeruitburen

▲ Gerard Unger, the typeface for the Dutch
road signs, 1997, ANWB.

22 Ergonomics

To extract meaning from lines of typeset text, readers use their eyes and brain, to which the shapes of typographic signs and their applications have no doubt been adapted. Although this field of inquiry is usually treated as part of legibility research, it is also part of ergonomics: 'the applied science of equipment design ... intended to maximize productivity by reducing operator fatigue and discomfort'.[1] Equipment design is here type design, the operator is the reader, and productivity can be understood as how much is comprehended of a text in relation to ease and speed of reading. Basically ergonomics is about making things we use easy to use, such as a mouse that fits the hand comfortably or a chair that does not cause back trouble.

Type designers are also readers. It is safe to assume that even the earliest punchcutters, including Johannes Gutenberg (c. 1397–1468), could read. To a certain extent they design what they like to read. This is reciprocity at work: you have learned to read and have come to appreciate certain letterforms – for the earliest punchcutters these were certain kinds of handwriting. These experiences are externalized and reflected in the letterforms you make, in their proportions, details, and in the sizes for text and display [see chapter 17]. Especially for sustained or immersive reading, type designers have, like other readers, become accustomed to seemingly permanent shapes, sizes, structures, textures, patterns and rhythms, agreeable to the eyes and the brain.

Typefaces with x-heights between 1.4 mm and 14 mm are, at a distance of 40 cm from the eyes to a page or screen, the extremes of a range of sizes that can be read fluently or easily and speedily, a conclusion that applies both to contemporary and historical type designs.[2] *Adobe Caslon* roman (1990–1992), designed by Carol Twombly (1959), has at 11 point an x-height of 1.6 mm, which in a book makes for comfortable reading at normal reading distance. At 70 cm from screen to eye, the type size and x-height should consequently be bigger, and older readers probably have to bring a chair closer to the screen or a book closer to their eyes.

In addition to the correlation between type size and reading distance, rhythm and reading distance also cooperate. The distance between the two verticals of *Adobe Caslon*'s 11 point roman **n** is approximately 0.8 mm and an **n** and **e** are about 0.5 mm apart. With such dimensions *Adobe Caslon* provides a pleasant rhythm [see chapter 12]. It is an alternation of black and white elements similar to that of many other typefaces, which suits the resolution of the photoreceptors in the retina.[a] This, of course, also applies to type size. Type has to be very small or condensed to go below the resolution threshold of the retina and to become difficult or impossible to read.

While type is being designed, the forms appearing on screen or paper are checked, shaped and reshaped by hand, guided by the designers' eyes and brain. Letterforms have come to an ergonomic conformity with the eyes and the brain; to a large extent this had already happened when writing and reading were in their early development, as in Mesopotamia around 3200 BC.[3] Letterforms have since then been adjusted and refined, in conjunction with the grammar of legibility [see chapter 3]: for example, in the later part of the eighth century with the development of the Carolingian minuscule, when letterforms, wordspaces, character size, line length, and many aspects of layout were brought into balance.[4]

A much further reaching proposition is that the functioning of the human brain and eyes have been instrumental in shaping the characters of not only the Latin script, but of all scripts: 'All rely on a small inventory of basic shapes'.[5] 'All provide the retina's fovea with a high-density concentration of optimally contrasted black-on-white marks. This format probably optimizes the amount of visual information that our retina and visual areas can transmit in a single eye fixation.'[b] This 'small inventory of basic shapes' or strokes that is apparently fundamental to all scripts is especially interesting. Whether these basic marks look anything like the invariant representations of letters extracted by the brain's letterbox is not clear [see chapter 6]. They may be related to the 'limited sequence of related strokes, which the pen ... ensures are all related to each other', which form the basis of formalized handwriting [see chapter 9], also for other scripts than the Latin.[c] Anyway, it looks like the brain and the eyes have made clear to scribes, punchcutters, and type designers which elements contribute to effective writing and pleasurable or comfortable reading, and to the design of letterforms that are easy to use.

If this is correct and the interaction of brains, eyes, and hands has led to written signs relying on this small inventory of basic shapes, then the comparison of a few scripts, for example Greek, Gujarati, and Arabic, already makes clear how much diversity such fundamental marks allow for. They also left room for changes through time, as written signs were handed down from one civilisation to another, taken by one people from another, or were pressed into service for another language than they originally served.

a] Oyster (1999), pp 82–90. This alternation of black and white elements can also be expressed as 'spatial frequency'. See: Legge (2011), the chapter titled: 'Spatial-Frequency Representation of Letters'.

b] Dehaene (2009), p 174. The fovea is the small part of the retina with which we can see a span of two to four characters with acuity. In a fixation, between saccades (eye movements) across a line of text, the eyes pick up from four to about eighteen characters, including spaces between words. The eyes pick up only a few characters if a text presents difficulties and more when it is easier to read, in terms of legibility as well as content (the way an author has handled a text).

c] Clayton (2013), p 115. Seemingly related to the 'small inventory of basic shapes' is the theory that elements of letterforms are based on things seen before you learn to read, on 'proto-letters', and that these help you while learning to read. See Dehaene (2009), p 137.

Ergonomics have not always been a matter of bare necessities or elementary utility. Most objects made by humans, especially signs for communication, have been cultivated, detailed, and refined, from cave paintings to letterforms on screens. In this process a preference for subtlety and even complexity seems to have prevailed.

1. http://www.thefreedictionary.com/ergonomics (20/02/2017).
2. Legge (2011), *passim*.
3. Senner (1989), p 43.
4. Gumbert (1993), *passim*.
5. Dehaene (2009), pp 173–179.

After age 40, the single pair of glasses or contact lenses you previously wore generally will no longer give you clear vision at all distances — or at least not without some compromises.

These vision problems are caused by *presbyopia*, which affects all of us beginning in middle age and reduces our ability to see at all distances.

Many vision correction options are available, such as presbyopia surgery and multifocal contact lenses or eyeglasses. If you need cataract surgery, you also have the option of choosing multifocal intraocular lenses to restore your ability to see at all distances.

If you are nearsighted, you have an advantage when you reach your 40s. Once presbyopia occurs, nearsighted eyes still see well up-close — if you remove your eyeglasses. Of course, with your glasses removed, distance vision is blurred. So you will need to put your glasses back on to see clearly across the room.

પડે એમ નથી. તરત જ એ બોલ્યો : 'મહારાજ, ભલે એ વ્રત આજથી હું લઉં છું.' વ્રત લીધું ને બીજે દિવસે ભાઈને દારૂ પીવા જવાની ઈચ્છા થઈ; પણ વ્રત યાદ આવ્યું. દારૂ પીધા પછી કેફમાં જૂઠું બોલાઈ ગયું તો? તો તો સાચું બોલવાનું વ્રત લીધું છે એ તૂટે. જુગારની ઈચ્છા થઈ, વ્યભિચારનો વિચાર આવ્યો. પણ મનને થયું કે એ બધામાં સાચું બોલીને આગળ ચાલવું મુશ્કેલ છે. પણ ચોરી કરવા ગયા વગર તો છૂટકો જ ન હતો. ચોરી વગર ખાવું શું? એણે ખૂબ વિચાર કરી જોયો. અંતે નક્કી કર્યું કે ચોરી કરવી પણ એવી કરવી કે પછી એમાંથી આખી જિંદગી ગુજારો થઈ શકે. એક વાર ચોરી કરી આવીને પછી ઘરમાં બેઠાબેઠા ખાવું. બહાર નીકળીએ તો જૂઠું બોલવું પડે ને? ચોરી પણ એવાને ઘેર કરવી કે જેની પાસે સૌથી વધુ ધન હોય. એવો તો કોણ હોય? લાવ, રાજાને ત્યાં જ ખાતર પાડું એમ કરી એ નીકળ્યો. રસ્તામાં સિપાઈ

▲ *Caslon*, 1990–1992, Adobe.

▲ *Keri Gujarati* (2012) by Kalapi Gajjar-Bordawekar. MA Typeface Design of the University of Reading.

23 Classifications

Classification is seen as a means of controlling the abundance of typefaces with widely differing characteristics, and for 'identifying, choosing and combining typefaces';[1] although there are different approaches to classifying typefaces. The *Encyclopedia of Type Faces*, originally published in 1953, lists seven categories: Roman Faces, Sans Serif Faces, Egyptian or Antique Faces, Outline, Shaded and Three-dimensional Letters, Decorated Types, Script Types. The first category is subdivided into: Venetian, Old Face, Transitional, Modern, Twentieth Century, Calligraphic, Display, Fat Faces, and Privately-held Types.[2] Like other classifications this one is arranged according to a mixture of criteria: history (Venetian, Twentieth Century), form (Sans Serif Faces, Outline), writing instruments (Calligraphic, Script Types), or added elements (Decorated Types). This is an outdated approach anyway.

A classification published in 1954 by the French typographer Maximilien Vox (1894–1974) was accepted in 1962 by the Association Typographique Internationale (ATypI) and in 1967 as a British Standard.[3] The original version counts nine classes: Manuaires, Humanes, Garaldes, Réales, Didones, Mécanes, Linéales, Incises and Scriptes – again a mixture of groups based on gestures and instruments (Manuaires, Incises),[a] on historical persons (Garaldes, Didones),[b] or on form (Linéales).[c]

A rare, unambiguous classification, although not intended as such, was devised by Gerrit Noordzij – purely morphological and based on his concepts of 'translation' and 'expansion' as consequences of using the broad-nibbed and pointed pen respectively [see chapter 4].[4] This covered only a part of all type designs but Indra Kupferschmid (1973–) has made it into a more comprehensive classification by adding the round-tipped pen[5] as the source for monolinear and geometric letterforms, while 'decorative' and 'blackletter'(Gothic;[d] Gebrochene Schriften) had to be added as categories to make this approach exhaustive.[6] Of all classifications that have been developed so far, this one is the most consistent.

a] 'Manuaires' show the hand of the designer who held the pen, brush, or another instrument, and 'Incises' show traces of the chisel, graver, and similar instruments.

b] 'Garaldes' is the combination of the surname of Claude Garamond and the first name of Aldus Manutius, while 'Didones' clearly refers to the Didot family and a little to Giambattista Bodoni as well.

c] 'Linéales' are linear type designs, sanserifs, either with or without a contrast.

d] Not to be confused with either the script for the Gothic language nor with Gothic as the label for some sanserifs.

Optima (1958) by Hermann Zapf, which is difficult to pigeonhole, is classed in the *British Standard Classification of Typefaces* together with *Gill Sans* (1928) as 'Humanist', within the larger group of 'Moderns' – amazing because moderns have a vertical contrast and 'humanist' is really old face (diagonal contrast).[7] Furthermore, *Optima* has a marked contrast between thick and thin strokes while *Gill Sans* comes close to monolinearity. In Indra Kupferschmid's classification *Optima* correctly appears in the group of sanserifs with contrast (Serifenlose mit Strichkontrast) positioned vertically (Statisches Formprinzip; modern face). The capitals of *Optima* are famously based upon early fifteenth-century Florentine interpretations of Romanesque capitals,[8] which were chiselled in stone, making *Optima* a member of the Incises of the Vox classification. Otherwise they are definitely humanist, with the modern lowercase beautifully complementing these capitals.

Classifications are intended to bring order and clarity to what must be for many a huge, intricate, and perplexing mass of typefaces. However, classifications are often complicated and unwieldy, more theoretical than practical, which limits their usefulness for the evaluation and selection of type designs.[9]

To come to grips with at least a large part of all type designs available at present, you can start with any publication showing many typefaces, either printed or on the web, preferably with descriptions.[10] By comparing and selecting, you will find favourites and may want to put into words why you fancy them. It helps if you limit your choices to, say, twenty typefaces for different purposes, and from different classes, times, and designers. If you find a design you like better than an earlier choice, then swap it for the latter. This will improve the critical eye.

....

1. https://www.fonts.com/content/learning/fontology/level-1/type-anatomy/type-classifications (14/06/2017).
2. Turner Berry (1962), p 7.
3. https://en.wikipedia.org/wiki/Vox-ATypI_classification (14/06/2017).
4. Noordzij (1982), pp 11, 14–18.
5. https://en.wikipedia.org/wiki/Speedball_(art_products) (08/06/2017).
6. Kupferschmid (2003), pp 30–44.
7. https://en.wikipedia.org/wiki/Vox-ATypI_classification#Lineal (18/06/2017).
8. Unger, 2013, pp 23, 24.
9. Dixon, 1995.
10. For example: Bringhurst (1996), pp 199–270, 'Prowling the specimen books', or Seddon (2016), pp 99–185.

....

ORIGINE, TRANSFORMATION & CLASSIFICATION
de la
LETTRE D'IMPRIMERIE
DÉTERMINÉES
par son

La Minuscule.

EMPATTEMENT

LES QUATRE GRANDES FAMILLES CLASSIQUES

Le ROMAIN ELZÉVIR	Le ROMAIN DIDOT	L'ANTIQUE	L'ÉGYPTIENNE
A EMPATTEMENT *TRIANGULAIRE*	EMPATTEMENT *A TRAIT FIN HORIZONTAL*	SANS EMPATTEMENT	EMPATTEMENT *RECTANGULAIRE*
Alphabet minuscule extrait de la *Caroline romane* et adapté à l'empattement des capitales romaines d'inscription par NICOLAS JENSON à la fin XV° siècle.	Transformation de la minuscule romaine d'après le principe d'empattement innové par GRANDJEAN dans son *romain du roi* et généralisé par F.-A. DIDOT au XVIII° siècle.	Adoption de la forme romaine de l'alphabet de NICOLAS JENSON pour l'ajouté d'une minuscule au type primitif des majuscules phéniciennes.	Adoption de la forme romaine de l'alphabet de NICOLAS JENSON pour l'ajouté d'une minuscule aux majuscules des inscriptions grecques.
	m	m	m
Minuscule *Elzévir*.	Minuscule *Didot*.	Minuscule *Antique*.	Minuscule *Égyptienne*.
Sous-Familles :			
Les LATINES	*CLASSIQUE DIDOT*	*REMARQUE.* — Aucun dessin d'alphabet de lettres d'imprimerie ne peut se soustraire à la loi de l'empattement et quel qu'on puisse l'imaginer, il contiendra fatalement dans ses terminaisons de jambages, sa coupe et sa graisse, des éléments-types de classement.	*ÉGYPTIENNE Anglaise*
			m
Empattement triangulaire horizontal adapté à la graisse de corps de l'Égyptienne angl. —	*Ajouté d'empattements triangulaires, maintien de la finesse des déliés.*		*Arrondissement intérieur des angles d'empattement.* —
			Sous-Famille :
Les DE VINNE HELLÉNIQUES TRAITS de PLUME L'AURIOL			*Les ITALIENNES*
Empattements elzé-viriens avec reprises horizontales. — *Traits bi-concaves, empattements tri-angulaires.* — *Empattements tri-angulaires au ca-lame.* — *Empattements tri-angulaires au pinceau.* —			*Empattements renforcés; traits intérieurs amaigris.*

▲ An early attempt to classify typefaces.
Actual size.
From: Francis Thibaudeau, *Manuel français de typo-graphie moderne*, 1924, Au Bureau de l'Édition.

Keleem rugs are made from 100% organic hand-spun wool, using natural dyes from plant sources that generate varying shades and hues.

Slight colour differences, size variations and irregularities may occur as a result of the hand woven process. These are the properties that make a handwoven rug special. Also available in:

Cherry Red
Moss Green
Mustard Yellow
Hazel Brown
Fern Green

▲ *Optima*, 1953, Stempel.

24 Evaluation

For a discussion of type designs prior to an evaluation, many of the necessary terms and descriptions of features can be found in the preceding chapters, such as: with or without serifs; light, bold, narrow, or wide; with a large or a small x-height and with short or long ascenders & descenders; roman and italic; with contrast or monolinear; with a strong, an average or a light colour; and many more. Such a discussion does not have to be anything in the nature of a wine-tasting with special rituals and language; it is the unfamiliarity of many with the details, distinctive features and general impressions of typefaces that can complicate such a discussion. Detailed terminology, descriptions of features, or 'tips to aid identification' of typefaces, combined with illustrations, can be found in many publications.[1]

For the evaluation of type designs, four main qualities can be derived from all the features and attributes described so far: 1 – the functionality, the fitness for a particular purpose or application; 2 – the social quality, dependent on convention, and on reading as a widely observed practice; 3 – the creative quality, the degree of originality and imagination, and the relationship with design in general and the visual arts; 4 – the expressive quality, eliciting emotive responses from readers, corresponding with a specific subject-matter.

1   Type designs can be made for specific contents, to meet clearly described functions, for example in response to requirements as formulated by a client, or a concept devised by the designer. Many typefaces, however, can convey all kinds of content: a dictionary, for example, as a resource for reference, performs a very different task from a political statement, although both can function with the same typeface, with a multi-purpose design. However, although the idea of a single typeface, or just a few, for all texts has had its proponents, variety is desirable to distinguish and avoid confusion.[a] With printed objects, page size, thickness, weight, kind of paper, and binding all contribute to diversity and distinction; while on screens, variety depends to a large extent on the individuality of typefaces.

a] Massimo Vignelli is quoted on the cover of *Emigre* magazine, number 18, 1991: 'In the new computer age the proliferation of typefaces and type manipulations represents a new level of visual pollution threatening our culture. Out of thousands of typefaces, all we need are a few basic ones, and trash the rest.'

2   The social quality is largely due to convention, connecting all who can write and read, and legibility can contribute to this with ease

of decoding for as large a group of readers as possible. Convention then guarantees a basic degree of recognizability and familiarity and is rarely infringed upon, although type designers like to explore its boundaries. Experiments with legibility often limit numbers of readers, while a particular type design with unconventional characteristics can function as a code within a group, for example for lovers of heavy-metal music.

3   Creativity is, in connection with type design, the ability to make original, imaginative and attractive letterforms, or shapes that arouse curiosity.[b] This view of creativity seemingly clashes with convention, but both have always been combined. The history of type design can be seen as the search for possibilities to synthesize the received letterforms with personal interpretations of these. So, originality can be a relatively limited quality in type design, especially, as stated earlier, with the design of typefaces for immersive reading, for use in small sizes and large quantities of text. Nevertheless, many designers have succeeded in bringing novel aspects even to this tough category of typefaces. One dictionary meaning of creative is: 'characterized by sophisticated bending of the rules or conventions',[2] which appears to be particularly applicable to type design.

b] It is estimated that over a hundred different definitions of creativity can be found in the literature. https://en.wikipedia.org/wiki/Creativity (05/06/2017).

Originality is also limited when new typefaces are clearly based on previous designs [see chapter 7]. Designs by predecessors, or aspects thereof, often serve as starting points for subsequent designs, and so one can be inspired or guided by, or be a follower of predecessors, in which case it is better to be conscious of one's examples, instead of using them unwittingly. Imitation, copying, and piracy have regrettably always been part of type design. The Intertype Corporation (founded in 1911 as the International Typesetting Machine Company), which manufactured a typesetting machine similar to the Linotype, listed typefaces for many years in its type specimens under the title: 'Intertype (or Fototronic) "look-alikes"'. Among many designs presented in two columns, one titled 'Intertype Identification' and the other 'Comparable to', were Hermann Zapf's *Palatino* (1949) as *Elegante*, and *Univers* (1957) by Adrian Frutiger as *Galaxy*.[3]

Type design has always been linked to and influenced by what is created in other branches of design (graphic, 3D, and industrial design), and in the arts and architecture. Developments in the arts, with movements such as Neoclassicism from approximately the mid-eighteenth century onward, or Constructivism and Neoplasticism

(Mondrian) in the twentieth century, have had a strong influence on type design and typography. In the early decades of the twenty-first century, type design reflects the diversity in art and design, the search for multiple ways to represent what is happening around us and to us. In the professional literature, these relationships have remained rather underexposed because type design and typography have often been treated as self-contained subjects, historically, theoretically, and practically.[c]

4   The expressive side of type has been discussed extensively, revealing how uncertainties can accompany this aspect regarding interpretations by readers. Broadly interpretable concepts seem to function best, such as friendly, inviting, open, lively, or serious. The expressive quality also has a social side, with letterforms being familiar, inviting or reassuring. It can similarly be argued that the expressive quality is close to the functional quality, that expressivity is in fact an important function of type designs.

c] Some of the publications in which type design and typography are related to other areas of design and the arts are: *The Letter as a Work of Art* (1951) by G. Knuttel, *Anatomy of Printing* (1970) by John Lewis, *Lettering in Architecture* (1975) by Alan Bartram, *Words and Buildings* (1980) by Jock Kinneir. And in Jan Tschichold's famous book *Die neue Typographie* (1928) there is a chapter on 'the new art' ('Die neue Kunst', pp 3–52), and also in the chapter on the history of the new typography ('Zur Geschichte der neuen Typographie', pp 52–65) reference is made to Futurism, Dadaism, De Stijl and Constructivism.

Typefaces can be evaluated from three perspectives: that of the designer, of those who select typefaces, and of those who read them. Readers can nowadays have a complex relationship with letterforms: as users of devices with a font menu they can compare, evaluate and select typefaces intentionally, while during reading they process letterforms nearly involuntarily. Large numbers of readers also find themselves scrutinizing formal letterforms on screen while keyboarding (processing words), as many do on a daily basis. They may look past the visible signs while writing, though, paying more attention to the content than to the letterforms.

As very familiar and everyday objects, letters pass to some extent beneath our notice[4] – at least in small sizes, in a fair amount of text, and when reading is immersive [see chapters 17 and 21]. This recalls Beatrice Warde's (1900–1969) comparison of reading with looking through a window: a plain-glass window – a text set in an unobtrusive typeface – will give you an unimpeded view, while a stained-glass window – a text set with a typeface that draws attention to itself – will obscure the view.[d] This comparison implies a judgment: only plain and self-effacing or very conventional typefaces and typography are correct; the subtitle of Beatrice Warde's essay (1956) is *Printing Should Be Invisible*. This leaves designers of text faces apparently with little freedom to manoeuvre, while there clearly is room for distinction, for features that, for

d] Warde (1956), pp 11–17. In 1927 Beatrice Warde became editor of the Monotype Recorder, and later she was the publicity manager of the Monotype Corporation.

example, catch the attention in large type sizes and dissolve into an attractive texture in small sizes [see chapter 17].

It has been stated that, on the one hand, everyday tasks, such as getting up, brushing teeth, breakfasting, or getting to work, are routine, 'requiring little thought or planning' and are shallow or narrow. Unusual activities, on the other hand, 'which require much thought and effort ... [are] wide and deep'.[5] Reading clearly is an everyday activity and seems to be narrow – although it can more aptly be described as a narrowing activity, making you focus and taking up most if not all of your attention, with the exclusion of other perceptions or activities. At the same time it is a deep task, bringing about much activity in the brain: recognizing letters, comprehending words, sentences, and discourse, relating newly incoming information and ideas with previous knowledge, and ample thought in general.

It is this combination of the everyday and depth which complicates evaluating type designs, getting an impression and forming an opinion during reading. On the one hand, letterforms are passed over quickly by readers on their way to what words and sentences communicate. On the other hand, letterforms have things to say for themselves, on behalf of the designer and of anyone who has selected the typeface and put it to work in typography. Even if a typographer or website designer goes for Beatrice Warde's unobtrusiveness, then that is a statement, an opinion that matters to readers. However, the actual course of things is that many different typefaces, many variations of letterforms, influence and enrich reading experiences every day – the operative word is multiplicity.

These reading experiences are weighed by readers, although it is hard to find out to what extent. Type designers and all who select typefaces assume that readers do take notice of the features of type designs and their possible expressive meanings. Characteristics of typefaces set in small sizes and presenting fair amounts of text may be evaluated insofar as readers are aware of them. When letters are large and texts are short and offer time for contemplation, then readers decidedly perceive details.

Professionals, with a training in typography, look at type designs in a different way than readers, even if the latter can choose fonts deliberately from a font menu. The professionals probably have background information about a type design they consider, about its history, the designer, in which genre of publication it often appears, what to conform to in connection with this knowledge and what to avoid, etcetera. Most readers will judge more impulsively and base choices on gut feelings.[6] So, if a designer selects *Franklin Gothic* (1902) for a headline, thinking of it as one of the great and powerful sanserifs of the twentieth century, readers possibly see an agreeable typeface but might want a more expressive design, or a more familiar one like *Arial* (1982).

Usually readers encounter typefaces chosen by others, by the professionals mentioned above, many of whom follow the dictates of their trade. Designers of newspapers and magazines will often choose seriffed faces for body copy, convinced that they are responding to readers' expectations – just as website designers are when choosing sanserifs. Typefaces chosen by typographic professionals are more or less imposed on readers, who may appreciate the choice, dislike it, or be indifferent – all in all, another process with many uncertainties. So the question is: are the qualities type designers equip their typefaces with correctly appreciated and valued by those who select the typefaces, and how many of these qualities are fathomed by readers?

During the design process, type designers continually contemplate, try out, reject, select, and adapt features. Most of these will be interpreted and evaluated by those who select typefaces, and eventually by readers. With a high degree of convention [see chapter 6], a type design will impress itself on those selecting it and on those reading it as familiar, and there is a fair chance that it will get used in book design. Although the terms 'old face' and 'modern face' will mean nothing to most readers, their visual consequences will play a role in the appreciation of a typeface, and so will a high or a low contrast, geometry, narrow, wide, angular or round letterforms. Readers are possibly unaware of features such as consistency, coherence, an agreeable rhythm or proper optical adjustments, as long as reading goes smoothly.

This interaction between type designers, graphic designers, and readers becomes really complicated when the emotional or expressive aspects of type are considered with the aim of controlling them. Type designers have little sway over interpretations of their intentions. Often a trend or a fashion, a prevailing style, takes over, which is not a problem if the letterforms have a voice that speaks to readers in the right tone at the right time. Novelty can do this trick, and so can a remix of existing and well-known features.

To what extent do aesthetic preferences play a role? Opinions such as those of Jan Tschichold about the letterforms of Claude Garamond – 'unsurpassable ... delightful and ... excellent'[7] – and of Eric Gill about the Roman square capitals – 'of such pre-eminent rationality and dignity'[8] – held sway for a considerable period. Other exemplars could be added: for example, the vigorous Baroque capitals of Hendrik van den Keere, cut between 1574 and 1580.[9] There are undeniably beautiful type designs in the modern-classical tradition, such as *Trinité* (1982) by Bram de Does (1934–2015). But to maintain that certain kinds of letterforms from antiquity or the Renaissance are more beautiful or qualitatively better than others does not seem to add much to a discussion about evaluation. Appreciating and classifying type designs on account of their excellence or beauty is often personal and prone to changes over time.

As mentioned before, many type designs share comparable qualities, are equally pleasing to the eyes and the mind, with properties such as harmonious proportions, an agreeable overall impression, authenticity, and more. To choose from such equivalents and to make choices in general, the four qualities mentioned at the beginning of this chapter can all be brought into action; then the operative word is inclusiveness. Sometimes a personal preference for a long-time favourite can prevail: the famous book designer Irma Boom (1960–) often uses *Plantin* (1913), thinking of it as a robust typeface, steady and decisive, carrying weight. She even thinks of it as modern, for example in the way its diacritics are deployed.[d] Otherwise, practical requirements, resulting perhaps from a discussion with a client, will yield criteria for the choice of a typeface or of several that can work together.

d] In an exchange of e-mails Irma Boom used the Dutch words: 'robuust, stoer, gedrongen, evenwichtig, modern, uitgesproken, zwart'. (22/05/2017)

The four qualities are never equally represented in a type design, usually differing in influence. This contributes to diversity, while distinguishing and analyzing these values can lead to thoughtful, reasoned and clear choices, both while creating a type design and when fonts are selected.

1. Useful publications are: Seddon (2016), *passim*; https://designschool.canva.com/blog/typography-terms/ (12/06/2017); https://www.fontshop.com/glossary (18/06/2017).
2. https://en.wikipedia.org/wiki/Creativity#Definition (05/06/2017).
3. https://hiveminer.com/Tags/intertype/Timeline (05/06/2017).
4. Forsey (2013), p 232.
5. Norman (2002), p 124.
6. Hyndman (2017), p 32.
7. Tschichold (1992), p 336.
8. Gill (1954), p 28.
9. Vervliet (1968), pp 224, 225.

ABC
DEFGHI
KLMN
OPQ R
STVX
YZ

▲ Hendrik van den Keere, 2-line Great Primer
Capitals (2 regelen Text), cut between 1574
and 1580. Actual size.

Evaluation can help you identify
Evaluation can help you identify
Evaluation can help you identify
Evaluation can help you identify
Evaluation can help you identify

It involves collecting and analyzing information about a program's activities, characteristics, and outcomes. Its purpose is to make judgments about a program, to improve its effectiveness, and/or to inform programming decisions.

It is important to periodically assess and adapt your activities to ensure they are as effective as they can be. Evaluation can help you identify areas for improvement and ultimately help you realize your goals more efficiently. Additionally, when you share your results about what was more and less effective, you help advance environmental education.

But Biddy's eyes were blazing so hard as she confronted Betty, and Betty was defending herself so heatedly that neither saw or heard Brown Owl.

'Whatever *is* the matter?' she demanded again.

The two turned angry faces to her.

'Betty promised to bring an extra cup.'

'I didn't! *You* did.'

'I never!'

'It looks as if I should have to ask the Brown Owl to go away when she comes,' remarked Brown Owl No. 3.

'Why?' The idea was so awful that the two stopped quarrelling to unite in their horror.

'Why?' they challenged again.

'You don't look as if you could turn into Golden Hand Brownies. All you look like is two turkey cocks.'

▲ *Trinité*, 1982, Autologic, The Enschedé Font Foundry.   ▲ *Plantin*, 1913, Monotype.

25 Epilogue: personal preferences

In 1976 Romanesque capitals struck me in the cloister of Moissac, north-west of Toulouse, in an inscription with the date the monastery was built, 1100, and the name of the principal, abbot Ansquetil. These curious letterforms and their amazing interaction intrigued me, but they had to wait. At the time I was working on *Demos* (1976) and *Praxis* (1977) and wanted to keep up with far-reaching changes in the graphic industry, such as the transition from hot-metal typesetting and letterpress printing to photo- and digital typesetting, and printing in offset (lithography). Such developments led, beside other type designs, to the creation of *Swift* in the early 1980s, while it took till 2003 for the Romanesque capitals to return to my attention.

Swift (1985) grew out of a long-time interest in newspapers, which suffered from the technological changes in terms of print quality. Around 1980 the two most common newspaper typefaces (particularly in Northwestern Europe), *Excelsior* (1931) and *Times New Roman* (1932), had both deteriorated from firmly printed metal letterforms into blurred images: contours became rounded off and the sharp serifs of *Times New Roman* were sometimes half gone at small sizes in the columns of newspapers. *Excelsior*'s serifs remained largely intact but were too heavy for my liking. After a series of sketches and tests I decided to fit out *Swift* with an overall sharpness or angularity, and with such strong serifs that these could not be ruined.

Actually *Excelsior* and *Times* were not so much examples for *Swift* as were a few other type designs, although *Times* provided the concept of a somewhat compressed design that does not look condensed, and the sturdiness of *Excelsior* was adopted to some extent. Otherwise *Plantin* (1913), *Vendôme* (1952) by François Ganeau (1912–1983) and Roger Excoffon, and *Trump Medieval* (1954) by Georg Trump all inspired me, along with an unpublished type design by William A. Dwiggins, *Experimental No. 223* (c.1936–1944).[a] *Plantin* is an old favourite as a reliable all-rounder, *Vendôme* I knew from holidays in France with my parents during my younger years, and *Trump Medieval* I encountered when I became interested in literature in secondary

a] Unger (1981), *passim*. In the autumn of 1979 I was asked to teach type design and typography for three months at the Rhode Island School of Design in Providence, Rhode Island. I used this opportunity to study Dwiggins's work in the Boston Public Library and in the Margaret I. King Library of the University of Kentucky, and in his former studio in Hingham near Boston, when his former assistant, Dorothy Abbe, was still alive and well.

school. The horizontality of *Swift*, as in the flat, horizontal parts of curves in **d** and **n**, for example, has a background in Dwiggins's *Electra* (1935) and in *Sheldon* (1947) by Jan van Krimpen (1892–1958).

In 1937 Dwiggins wrote, preceding the design of *No. 223* and commenting on Linotype newspaper typefaces like *Ionic* (1925) and *Excelsior* (1931): 'I think very little can be added on the side of the problem that comes under the head: It Will Print. If anything more can be done, it will have to be in the department: It Can Be Read.'[1] When I read these words in 1979, I found them strongly motivating. Meanwhile, *Plantin*, *Trump Medieval* and *Vendôme* influenced the choice for an old-face approach, and *Vendôme* also contributed a sense of speed and sharp-edgedness, as of course did the birds after which *Swift* has been named – dark, letter-like silhouettes against the sky.

While *Swift* was being designed, it was clear that technologies for typesetting, reproduction and printing were steadily improving, and I did not want this type design, although built to cope with temporary technological restrictions, to be tied to these constraints. With improved technological circumstances, *Swift* still functions satisfactorily, with its characteristics now somewhat more noticeable in the small sizes.

With the advent of the digital age in type design, technology became stimulating rather than limiting, as with the possibility in OpenType to design contextual alternates.[2] This feature was ideally suited to *Alverata* (2013), the type design based on Romanesque inscriptions made between 1000 and 1200 ad, approximately.[3] In 2003, these medieval letterforms caught my attention again, and I began to systematically study Romanesque inscriptions spread across a large part of Europe. Unconventional letterforms were beckoning me.

In Romanesque capitals three kinds of letterforms were merged: descendants of Roman Imperial square capitals, uncials, and angular versions of round letters, a miscellany that originated in the British Isles. Roman capitals were used throughout the Roman Empire, also in England during the occupation by the Romans from 43 to 410 AD. Uncials were brought to England in 597 by Augustine of Canterbury (?–604), who was sent there from Rome on a Christianizing mission. And the angular versions of round letters have an Irish-Celtic background mixed with Anglo-Saxon elements (Insular art), and are influenced by the Ogham alphabet and runes.[4] In the seventh century this mixture appeared first in manuscripts and was taken to continental Europe by Irish-Scottish monks and Anglo-Saxon missionaries, including Willibrord (658–739) and Boniface (672–754).[b]

Early in 2008 I had made an inventory with digitizations of some of the many variants of Romanesque letterforms. It will never be possible to recover all of

b] Uncials and Roman capitals had been mixed earlier (see Morison, 1972, pp 90, 97–101), and uncials also reached northern-Europe across land over the Alps; but the mixture of roman capitals, uncials, and Celtic angular forms has had a much stronger influence in the opposite direction, from north to south.

these, as too many inscriptions have disappeared. From then on I worked simultaneously on a PhD thesis about the subject (finished in 2013) and on the type design. The latter required several major design decisions: one of these was a resolution to make the letterforms rich in contrast instead of rather monolinear, mainly inspired by a beautiful, very varied inscription on the west facade of Pisa cathedral. Some of the main characteristics were selected previously: gradual transitions from thick to thin parts, straight parts that widen towards their end and have short triangular serifs. Another decision was to regulate the application of variants. In a conventional typeface, the capitals are on the whole more angular than the lowercase, while the lowercase letters are generally rounder than the capitals. For the alternates of *Alverata* this arrangement was reversed, and I added some variants of my own, like my medieval colleagues often did.

After having considered an italic with some angular lowercase letters – which I didn't really like – the family was composed of three different upright versions, normal, informal, and irregular, with one italic. The normal version includes Greek and Cyrillic, and all these styles have been executed in six weights: light, regular, medium, semi-bold, bold, and black. The irregular houses the alternate letterforms.

Beside the ideas for *Swift* and *Alverata*, described above, some interests have influenced all my type designs, especially two movements in the arts: Modernism and Modern Classicism.[c] In 2006, for an exhibition in the Victoria & Albert Museum, Modernism was summarized as follows: 'It was not a style but a loose collection of ideas [that] ... shared certain underlying principles: a rejection of history and applied ornament, a preference for abstraction and a belief that design and technology could transform society.'[d] The rejection of history was wasted on me. Modern Classicism can be described as the twentieth-century continuation of the regard for aesthetic attitudes and principles from the arts and architecture of ancient Greece and Rome, and of the Renaissance. It is characterized by harmony, restraint, and clarity.[5] Both movements have had an impact on the arts and architecture far into the twentieth century, and also on typography and type design. I was exposed to both views during my education, to modernist designs by Piet Zwart (1885–1977) and Willem Sandberg (1897–1984), for example, and to the modern-classicist type designs of Jan van Krimpen.

In my first year in art school (1963) I was given Trajan capitals to copy, and if ever modern-classical numerals have been designed, fit to be combined with

c] In *Modern Typography* (1992), pp 52–66, Robin Kinross calls this movement 'New Traditionalism', a description apparently coined by Jan Tschichold (Burke, 2007, p 282). Tradition is 'a mode of thought or behaviour followed ... continuously from generation to generation'. With tradition there is little or no change in the transfer of ideas, while Classicism is a theme that allows interpretation and adaptation to individual insights and periods. – http://www.thefreedictionary.com/tradition (16/06/2017).

d] Wilk (2006). This quotation does not come from the catalogue but from a brochure accompanying this exhibition and the book.

Roman square capitals, then they are those on stamps (1946) by Van Krimpen, which I collected as a boy. Such instances, together with a predilection for abstraction, clarity, and even idealism, left me with a fondness of pure forms, such as *Le commencement du monde* (1924), a sculpture by Constantin Brancusi (1876–1957) or the painting *Blue Curve VI* (1982) by Ellsworth Kelly (1923–2015),[e] and more recently a necklace (2017), a deceptively simple chain, by Gijs Bakker (1942–). The links cannot be of a more straightforward shape, comparable to the conventional shapes of letters. They are all made of different materials and their varying sizes are the result of the specific weights of these materials; all links have the same weight – a very ingenious and original starting point. This chain shows how much variation a simple basic shape allows for.

e] The painting by Gris and the sculpture by Brancusi are both in the Kröller-Müller Museum, the Netherlands, and the painting by Kelly is in the Stedelijk Museum, Amsterdam.

All these abstract works of art have a rapport with letterforms – which are also totally abstract – and the counter spaces of letters. In both *Swift* and *Alverata*, and in other designs as well, I have been able to fully enjoy and to express this fondness in letterforms.[f]

f] The purest forms I have made as a type design are those of *Decoder* (1992).

The purpose of *Swift* was well defined: to be a messenger, a carrier of news, quick on its feet (and wings), clear and open, and with a dependable strength. The purpose of *Alverata* was to experiment, to find out what the new technological capabilities could offer me and whether ancient alternative letterforms could be turned into letterforms relevant to our times. Also, I had observed that many new type designs (around 2010) were low in contrast and had stubby serifs, which led me to react with a certain sharpness and short, triangular serifs. I had earlier developed this concept into *Amerigo* (1986), designed to cope with low-resolution laser printing (300 dpi) without hinting, while in *Alverata* this idea has been much refined. Otherwise, general considerations and ideas that play a role in most of my designs have recurred in *Alverata* too: clarity and good legibility, individuality, attractiveness, research, and experimentation.

1. Unger (1981), p 309.
2. http://ilovetypography.com/2011/04/01/engaging-contextuality/ (21/05/2017). https://glyph-sapp.com/tutorials/features-part-3-advanced-contextual-alternates (21/05/2017).
3. Unger (2013), *passim*.
4. Gray (1986), p 61.
5. This description is a combination of elements from: http://www.thefreedictionary.com/classicism and: https://en.oxforddictionaries.com/definition/classicism (both 16/06/2017).

▲ Inscription in the cloister of Moissac
from 1100.

Change involves many components.
Some, such as customers or competitors,
initiate or are the cause of change.

In other cases there are things that affect
the implementation of change, such as
processes and motivation.

SsSsSsSsSsSsSsSsSsSsSs
ssssSSSSSSSSSSSSSSSSSSss

triomphante aux bornes d'un empire
aboli, la lettre des pierres jalonne les
chemins des cohortes romaines, inscr
it le nom des procurateurs et des jug

triomphante aux bornes d'un empire aboli, la
lettre des pierres jalonne les chemins des coho
rtes romaines, inscrit le nom des procurateurs
et des juges au front des colonnes de gloire, sur
les dalles funèbres qui deviennent pour nous

≜ *Demos*, 1976, and *Praxis*, 1977.   ▲ *Vendôme*, 1952, Olive.

▲ *Swift*, 1985, Hell.

The offspring of two animals or plants of different breeds, varieties, species, or genera, especially as produced through human manipulation for specific genetic characteristics.

10 Point

How is one to assess and evaluate a type face in terms of its esthetic design? Why do the pace-makers in the art of printing rave over a specific face of type? What do they see in it? Why is it so superlatively pleasant to their eyes? Good design is always practical design. And what they see in a good type design is, partly, its excellent practical fitness to perform its work. It has a "heft" and balance in all of its parts just right for its size, as any good tool has. Your good chair has all of its parts made nicely to the right size to do exactly the work that the chair has to do, neither clumsy and thick, nor "skinny" and weak, no waste of material and no lack of strength. And, beyond that, the chair may have been made by a man who worked out in it his

But the best way to appreciate Dwiggins' mastery in this area is to study examples of his work, either at the memorial exhibitions, which doubtless will be shown throughout the country, or in public collections. To aid in identifying the large proportion of his work that is not signed, as complete a catalogue as possible should soon be compiled, while those who can distinguish it from imitations and can save it from being lost, are still on hand. Until one sees an exhibition like that in the Boston Public Library, one cannot realize how attractive and significant his private experiments, his incidental commissions really are. In these, more than anywhere else, Dwiggins shows his intimate connection with the manuscript tradition, which may well be carried further in the future, thanks to the inspiration of

≜ *Trump Medieval*, 1954, Weber.　　　　▲ *Electra*, 1935, Linotype

▲ *Experimental No. 223*, c. 1936–1944, Linotype, with capitals of *Excelsior*. Actual size.

Alzo kwam hij stillekens uit die bossige hoeken;
Hij scheurde een tak, dicht van bladeren overvloedig,
Zijn schamelheid te dekken, en gink hem doen verkloeken
Uit den bosse te treden, recht als een leeuwe moedig
Die op zijn krachten betrouwt, briesende verwoedig
Met verspreide klauwen uit het woud komt geschreden:
— 't Hoofd recht hij op en ziet met zijn vierige ogen gloedig
Na ossen schapen oft herten om die te ontleden;
Die spoort hij onversaagd te verscheuren tot allen steden
Door d'onschamele honger, dwingende tegens 't betamen —:
Zo kwam Ulysses na die eerbare maagden treden

a a a **a a a a a** a a a
b b b **b b b b b** b b b
c c c **c c c c c** c c c
d d d **d d d d d** d d d
e e e **e e e e e** e e e
f f f **f f f f f** f f f
g g g **g g g g g** g g g
h h h **h h h h h** h h h
i i i **i i i i i** i i i

▲ *Sheldon*, 1947, Monotype, Oxford University   ▲ *Alverata*, 2013, TypeTogether.
Press. Actual size.

ABCDE FGH
IKLMNOPQ
RSTVWX

AAAAAAA꓅

ꝺꝺꞓꞬꞬꞬꞬꞬ

ꝁꝁʜꝃꝁʟ

ꟽꟽꟽꟽꟽꟽꟽ

NNNꞐꞐOO

ꝘꝗꝗꝗRRRR

Sꙅꙅꞇꞇꞇꞇ

ꙋꙋꙋꙋxx

aneh aneh

▲ Inscription on the west facade of Pisa cathedral, first quarter of the twelfth century.

▼ Detail of the inscription on the west facade of Pisa cathedral.

afhuɛf

		informal	irregular
light	Alverata	Alverata	Alverata
light italic	*Alverata*		
regular	Alverata	Alverata	Alverata
italic	*Alverata*		
medium	Alverata	Alverata	Alverata
medium italic	*Alverata*		
semibold	**Alverata**	**Alverata**	**Alverata**
semibold italic	***Alverata***		
bold	**Alverata**	**Alverata**	**Alverata**
bold italic	***Alverata***		
black	**Alverata**	**Alverata**	**Alverata**
black italic	***Alverata***		

≜ Some of the main characteristics of Romanesque letterforms in inscriptions: straight parts that widen towards their end and have short triangular serifs, and gradual transitions from thick to thin parts.

▲ While capitals are on the whole more angular than the lowercase, and lowercase letters are generally rounder than the capitals, this arrangement was reversed for the alternates of *Alverata* – some examples.

▲ An overview of the family members of *Alverata*.

Briefkaart met betaald antwoord

verzonden:

ROTTERDAM
-3. VII. 12
1
1935

ROTTERDAM

BEEK (LB)
-4. VII. 17
1
1935

terug.

BEEK (LB)

Wanneer je iemand per briefkaart iets vraag en je wilt, dat hij je zoo vlug mogelijk za antwoorden, stuur dan een **briefkaart me betaald antwoord.**

De geadresseerde ontvangt jouw briefkaar met daaraan gehecht een gefrankeerde ant woordkaart; deze scheurt hij af, schrijft e zijn antwoord op en zendt hem aan je terug

Wanneer je niet per briefkaart maar per brie iemand iets vraagt, kun je in je brief een post zegel voor antwoord sluiten.

Dat gaat niet, wanneer degene aan wie j iets te vragen hebt in het buitenland woon Denk eens na, waarom dat niet gaat!

In zoo'n geval koop je op het postkantoor ee **antwoord-coupon** en sluit die bij je brie in. Die coupon kan in elk land ingewissel worden tegen een postzegel van dat land, di op de naar Nederland terug te zenden brie kan worden geplakt.

stedelijk museum

◀ Piet Zwart, *Het boek van PTT*, 1938, Hoofdbestuur der Posterijen, Telegrafie en Telefonie, 25.1 × 17.7 cm.

▲ Willem Sandberg, *9 years stedelijk museum Amsterdam*, 1954, 25.9 × 19 cm.

ABCDEFGHIJKLMN
OPQRSTUVWXYZ
&1234567890
abcdefghijklmnopqr
stuvwxyzij.,:;!?"'-(*[—
1234567890

▲ Jan van Krimpen, *Spectrum*, 1952, Joh. Enschedé en Zonen.

▲ Jan van Krimpen, standard numeral stamps, 1946, PTT, 2 × 2.5 cm each.

▲ Constantin Brancusi, *Le commencement du monde*, 1924, 16.5 × 28.5 × 15.5 cm.
COLLECTION KRÖLLER-MÜLLER MUSEUM, OTTERLO, THE NETHERLANDS

▲ Ellsworth Kelly, *Blue Curve VI*, 1982, 202 × 392 cm.
COLLECTION STEDELIJK MUSEUM AMSTERDAM, THE NETHERLANDS

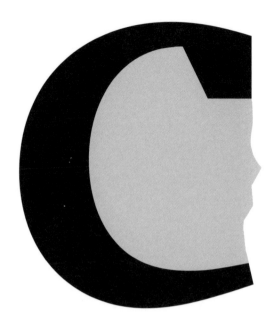

A homeland may also be referred to as a fatherland, a motherland, or a mother country, depending on the culture and language of the nationality in question.

◀ Gijs Bakker, *Necklace 3 Point 7*, 2014, 26.2 × 16 cm. PRIVATE COLLECTION

▲ The counter of the lowercase **c** of *Swift* semibold.

▲ *Amerigo*, 1986, Bitstream.

Bibliography

Abbe, D. – (1979). *Stencilled Ornament & Illustration*. Hingham MA: Püterschein-Hingham.

Allan, V.L. – (2007). *Theological Works of the Venerable Bede and their Literary and Manuscript Presentation, with Special Reference to the Gospel Homilies*. Oxford: Thesis for the degree of Master of Letters. https://tartarus.org/verity/thesis.html

Ambrose, G., P. Harris – (2005). *Typography (Basics Design)*. Lausanne: AVA Publishing.

Baines, P., A. Haslam – (2002). *Type & Typography*. London: Laurence King Publishing Ltd.

Barker, N. – (1974). The Aldine roman in Paris, 1530–1534, in: *The Library*, Vol. xxix, No. 1. Oxford: Oxford University Press.

Barmettler, R. – (2016). Swiss type design now, in: *Yearbook of Type*, No. 2. Zürich: Niggli.

Barton, D. – (2007). *Literacy*. Oxford: Blackwell Pubishing.

Bartram, A. – (1975). *Lettering in Architecture*. London: Lund Humphries.

Beaujon, P. – (1926). The 'Garamond' types, in: *The Fleuron*, No. 5. London: Cambridge University Press.

Beier, S. – (2012). *Reading Letters*. Amsterdam: bis Publishers.

Beier, S., M. Dyson – (2013). The influence of serifs on 'h' and 'i': useful knowledge from design-led scientific research, in: *Visible Language* 47.3. Cincinnati: University of Cincinnati.

Bessemans, A. – (2012). *Letterontwerp voor kinderen met een visuele functiebeperking*. Leiden: Doctoral thesis Leiden University.

Blumenthal, J. – (1935). The fitting of type, in: *The Dolphin*, No. 2. New York: The Limited Editions Club.

Boag, A. – (1996). Typographic measurement: a chronology, in: *Typography Papers*, No. 1. Reading: the Department of Typography & Graphic Communication, The University of Reading.

Brandt, D. – (2015). *The Rise of Writing*. Cambridge: Cambridge University Press.

Bringhurst, R. – (1996). *The Elements of Typographic Style*. Vancouver: Hartley & Marks.

Brody, N., J. Wozencroft – (2012). *Fuse*, No. 1–20. Köln: Taschen GmbH.

Brown, M. – (2002). *A Guide to Western Historical Scripts from Antiquity to 1600*. London: The British Library.

Bundscherer, M. – (2016). *Sprachsatz*. München: Privately published.

Burchartz, M. – (1953). *Gestaltungslehre*. München: Prestel-Verlag.

Burke, C. – (1992). Peter Behrens and the German letter: type design and architectural lettering, in: *Journal of Design History*. Vol. 5, No. 1. Oxford: Oxford University Press.

Burke, C. – (1998a). *Paul Renner*. London: Hyphen Press.

Burke, C. – (1998b). German hybrid typefaces 1900–1914, in: *Blackletter: type and national identity*. New York: Cooper Union.

Burke, C. – (2007). *Active Literature*. London: Hyphen Press.

Caflisch, M. – (1996). Von Skripten, in: *Typografische Monatsblätter*, Nr. 6. Bern: Gewerkschaft Druck und Papier.

Carter, H. – (2002). *A View of Early Typography*. Oxford: Oxford University Press.

Catich, E.M. – (1991). *The Origin of the Serif*. Davenport: Catich Gallery, St. Ambrose University.

Clayton, E. – (2013). *The Golden Thread*. London: Atlantic Books.

Cost, P.A. – (2011). *The Bentons*. Rochester: RIT Cary Graphic Arts Press.

Coulmas, F. – (1991). *The Writing Systems of the World*. Oxford: Basil Blackwell.

Culler, J. – (2000). *Literary Theory*. Oxford: Oxford University Press.

Crystal, D. – (1998). Toward a typographical linguistics, in: *Type: a Journal of the ATypI*, No. 2. New York: ATypI.

De Groot, L. – (2015). Kernologica, in: *365 x typo*. Paris: étapes: editions.

De Does, B. – (1982). *Trinité 1, 2, 3*. Lausanne: Autologic SA.

De Does, B. – (2013). *Trinité & Lexicon*. Amsterdam: De Buitenkant.

Dehaene, S. – (2003). Natural born readers, in: *New Scientist*, Vol. 179, No. 2402, London: Reed Business Information Ltd.

Dehaene, S. – (2009). *Reading in the Brain*. New York: Penguin Group.

De Vinne, T.L. – (1886). *Historic Printing Types*. New York: The Grolier Club.

De Vinne, T.L. – (1900). *A Treatise on the Processes of Type-making, the Point System, the Names, Sizes, Styles and Prices of Plain Printing Types*, a volume of *The Practice of Typography*. New York: The Century Co.

Di Sciullo, P. – (2006). *Pierre di Sciullo*. Paris: Pyramid.

Dixon, C. – (1995). Why we need to reclassify type, in: *Eye*, No. 19. London: Emap Business Communications Ltd.

Dreyfus, J. – (1952). *The Work of Jan van Krimpen*. Utrecht: W. de Haan.

Dreyfus, J. – (1982). *Aspects of French Eighteenth-Century Typography*. Cambridge: The Roxburghe Club.

Dwiggins, W.A. – (1935). *Emblems and Electra*. New York: Mergenthaler Linotype Company.

Dwiggins, W.A. – (1939). *Caledonia*. New York: Mergenthaler Linotype Company.

Dwiggins, W.A. – (1940). *WAD to RR: a Letter about Designing Type*. Cambridge MA: Harvard College Library.

Dyson, M., C.Y. Suen – (2016). *Digital Fonts and Reading*. Singapore: World Scientific Publishing Co.

Evans, H. – (1974). Handling newspaper text, in: *Editing and Design 2*, London: Heinemann.

Falk, W. – (1975). *Bokstavsformer och typsnitt genom tiderna*. Stockholm: Bokförlaget Prisma.

Filser, N. – (1975). *Pangramme: Learning Type Design*. Metz: École Supérieure d'Art de Lorraine.

Fiset, D. et al. – (2008). Features for identification of uppercase and lowercase letters, in: *Psychological Science*. Thousand Oaks, CA: Sage Publishing.

Fleischmann, G. – (1984). *Bauhaus: Drucksachen, Typografie, Reklame*. Düsseldorf: Edition Marzona.

Flor, M. – (2016). *Lust auf Lettering*. Mainz: Verlag Hermann Schmidt.

Flor, M. – (2017). *The Golden Secrets of Lettering.* New York. Princeton University Press.

Forsey, J. – (2013). *The Aesthetics of Design.* Oxford: Oxford University Press.

Forssman, F., R. de Jong. – (2002). *Detailtypografie.* Mainz: Verlag Hermann Schmidt.

Fournier, P.-S. – (1995). *The Manuel Typographique of Pierre-Simon Fournier le jeune.* Darmstadt: Technische Hochschule Darmstadt. (English translation by Harry Carter and an introduction by James Mosley).

Freeland, C. – (2001). *Art Theory: a Very Short Introduction.* Oxford: Oxford University Press.

Frutiger, A. – (1980). *Type Sign Symbol.* Zürich: ABC Verlag.

Gerstner, K. – (1968). *Programme entwerfen.* Teufen: Verlag Arthur Niggli.

Gill, E. – (1940). *Autobiography.* London: Jonathan Cape.

Gill, E. – (1954, originally 1931). *An Essay on Typography.* London: J. M. Dent & Sons Ltd.

Gineste, J. – (2010). Mistral, in: *Roger Excoffon et la Fonderie Olive.* Paris: Ypsilon.

Gray, N. – (1976). *Nineteenth Century Ornamented Typefaces.* London: Faber and Faber Ltd.

Gumbert, J.P. – (1993). 'Typography' in the manuscript book, in: *Journal of the Printing Historical Society.* No. 22, London.

Haiman, G. – (1983). *Nicholas Kis.* San Francisco: Jack W. Stauffacher / The Greenwood Press.

Hargreaves, G.D. – (1992). Florentine script, Paduan script, and roman type, in: *Gutenberg Jahrbuch,* Gutenberg-Gesellschaft, Mainz.

Hart, H. and several authors. – (2014). *New Hart's Rules.* Oxford: Oxford University Press.

Henestrosa, C., L. Meseguer, J. Scaglione. – (2017). *How to Create Typefaces.* Madrid: Tipo E.

Highsmith, C. – (2012). *Inside Paragraphs.* Boston: Font Bureau.

Hochuli, J. – (2015). *Detail in Typography.* Paris: Éditions B42.

Hulten, P. et al. – (1979). *Paris-Moscou 1900–1930.* Paris: Centre Georges Pompidou.

Hutt, A. – (1967). *Newspaper Design.* Oxford: Oxford University Press.

Hyndman, S. – (2017). Just your type, in: *'I'* (newspaper, 25/04/2017) Edinburgh: Johnston Press.

Jammes, A. – (1998). *Les Didot.* Paris: Agence culturelle de Paris.

Johnson, A.F. – (1959). *Type Designs.* London: Grafton & Co.

Johnston, A. – (2011). *Transitional Faces.* London: The British Library.

Johnston, E. – (1962). *Writing & Illuminating, and Lettering.* London: Sir Isaac Pitman & Sons Ltd.

Keedy, J. – (1990). Untitled, in: *Emigre,* No. 15. Berkeley ca: Emigre Graphics.

Kelly, R.R. – (1977). *American Wood Type: 1828–1900,* New York: Da Capo Press Inc.

Kinross, R. – (1992). *Modern Typography.* London: Hyphen Press.

Kinross, R. – (1997). Type as critique, in: *Typography papers,* No. 2. Reading: The Department of Typography & Graphic Communication, The University of Reading.

Kinneir, J. – (1980). *Words and Buildings.* London: The Architectural Press.

Knight, S. – (1998). *Historical Scripts.* New Castle de: Oak Knoll Press.

Knuttel, G. – (1951). *The Letter as a Work of Art.* Amsterdam: Amsterdam Type Foundry.

Kolers, P.A. – (1969). Clues to a letter's recognition, implications for the design of characters, in: *The Journal of Typographic Research,* Vol. III, No. 2, Cleveland: The Press of Western Reserve University.

Kudrnovská, L. – (2015). Something is going on in Latin America, in: *365 x typo*, Paris: etapes: editions.

Kupferschmid, I. – (2003). *Buchstabenkommenseltenallei n.* Zürich: Verlag Niggli.

Larson, K. – (2004). The science of word recognition, in: *Eye*, No. 52, Croydon: Quantum Business Media.

Legge, G.E., C.A. Bigelow – (2011). *Does Print Size Matter for Reading? A Review of Findings from Vision Science and Typography*. Washington: hhs Public Access.

Lewis, J. – (1970). *Anatomy of Printing*. London: Faber & Faber Ltd.

Licko, Z. – (1990). Untitled, in: *Emigre*. No. 52, Berkeley CA: Emigre Graphics.

Lidwell, W., K. Holden, J. Butler – (2015). *Universal Principles of Design*. Beverly MA: Rockport Publishers.

Lowry, M. – (1991). *Nicholas Jenson*. Oxford: Basil Blackwell.

Martin, J-H., et al. – (2015). *Herman de Vries: to be all ways to be*. Amsterdam: Valiz.

McLean, R. – (2012). *Jan Tschichold: Typographer*. London: Lund Humphries.

Middendorp, J. – (2004). *Dutch Type*. Rotterdam: 010 Publishers.

Middendorp, J. – (2011). *Shaping Text*. Amsterdam: BIS Publishers.

Mooney, A. – (2011). *Modularity: an Elemental Approach to Type Design*. Type Culture.

Moran, J. – (1971). *Stanley Morison: his Typographic Achievement*. London: Lund Humphries.

Morison, S. – (1926). Towards an ideal italic, in: *The Fleuron*. Cambridge: The University Press.

Morison, S. – (1930). First principles of typography, in: *The Fleuron*. Cambridge: The University Press.

Morison, S. – (1962). *On Type Designs Past and Present*. London: Ernest Benn.

Morison, S. – (1963). On the classification of typographical variations, in: *Type Specimen Facsimiles*. London: Bowes & Bowes Publishers Ltd.

Mosley, J. – (1964). Trajan revived, in: *Alphabet 1964*. London: James Moran Ltd.

Mosley, J. – (1999). *The Nymph and the Grot*. London: Friends of the St Bride Printing Library.

Mosley, J. – (2002). Les caractères de l'imprimerie royale, in: *Le Romain du Roi*. Lyon: Musée de l'imprimerie.

Moxon, J. – (1978). *Mechanick Exercises*. New York: Dover Publications, Inc.

Müller, L. – (2008). *Helvetica Forever*. Baden: Lars Müller Publishers.

Naegele, I., P. Eisele – (2012). *Texte zur Typografie, Positionen zur Schrift*. Zürich: Verlag Niggli.

Noordzij, G. – (1982). *The Stroke of the Pen*. The Hague: Koninklijke Academie van Beeldende Kunsten.

Noordzij, G. – (1985). *De streek: theorie van het schrift*. Zaltbommel: Van de Garde.

Noordzij, G. – (1988). *De staart van de kat*. Leersum: GHM.

Noordzij, G. – (2000). *De handen van de zeven zusters*. Amsterdam: Uitgeverij G.A. van Oorschot.

Norman, D.A. – (2002). *The Design of Everyday Things*. New York: Basic Books.

Osley, A. S. – (1972). *Luminario*. Nieuwkoop: Miland Publishers.

Osterer, H., P. Stamm – (2008). *Adrian Frutiger – Schriften. Das Gesamtwerk*. Basel: Birkhäuser.

Ovink, G.W. – (1938). *Legibility, Atmosphere-value and Forms of Printing Types*. Leiden: A.W. Sijthoff's Uitgeversmaatschappij n.v.

Ovink, G.W. – (1971a). Nineteenth-century reactions against the Didone type model – I, in: *Quærendo*. Vol 1, No. 2. Amsterdam: Theatrum Orbis Terrarum.

Ovink, G.W. – (1971b). Nineteenth-century reactions against the Didone type model – 2, in: *Quærendo*. Vol 1, No. 4. Amsterdam: Theatrum Orbis Terrarum.

Ovink, G.W. – (1972). Nineteenth-century reactions against the Didone type model – 3, in: *Quærendo*. Vol 2, No. 2. Amsterdam: Theatrum Orbis Terrarum.

Oyster C.W. – (1999) *The Human Eye*. Sunderland MA: Sinauer Associates, Inc.

Parkes, M.B. – (1992). *Pause and Effect: an Introduction to the History of Punctuation in the West*. Aldershot: Scolar Press.

Parkes, M.B. – (2008). Which came first, reading or writing?, in: *Their Hands Before Our Eyes: a Closer Look at Scribes*. Aldershot: Ashgate Publishing Ltd.

Petersen, A. – (2004). *Sandberg, Director + Designer of the Stedelijk*. Rotterdam: 010 Publishers.

Rayner, K., A. Pollatsek – (1989). *The Psychology of Reading*. Hillsdale: Lawrence Erlbaum Associates.

Re, M., et al. – (2003). *Typographically Speaking: the Art of Matthew Carter*. Baltimore County: Albin O. Kuhn Library & Gallery, University of Maryland.

Reed, T.B. – (1952). *A History of the Old English Letter Foundries*. London: Faber and Faber Ltd.

Reuß, R. – (2016). *Die perfekte Lesemachine*. Göttingen: Wallstein Verlag.

Reynolds, A.L. – (2017). Reputations: Nadine Chahine, in: *Eye*, No. 94. London: Eye Magazine Limited.

Rollins, C.P. – (1968). Reflections on the Century typeface, by T.L. De Vinne, in: *Theodore Low De Vinne*. New York: The Typophiles.

Ryder, J. – (1979). *The Case for Legibility*. London: The Bodley Head.

Sanocki, T., M.C. Dyson. – (2015). Letter processing and font information during reading: beyond distinctiveness, where vision meets design, in: *Attention, Perception & Psychophysics*. No. 74, Berlin: Springer Verlag.

Schreuders, P. – (1977). *Lay In Lay Out*. Amsterdam: Gerrit Jan Thiemefonds.

Seddon, T. – (2016). *Let's Talk Type*. London: Thames & Hudson.

Senner, W. (ed.) – (1989). *The Origins of Writing*. Lincoln NE: University of Nebraska Press.

Shaw, P. – (2015). *The Eternal Letter*. Cambridge MA: MIT Press.

Slimbach, R. – (1994). *Adobe Jenson: a Contemporary Revival*. San Jose CA: Adobe Systems Inc.

Slinn, J., S. Carter, R. Southall – (2014). *History of the Monotype Corporation*. London: Printing Historical Society; Woodstock: Vanbrugh Press.

Smeijers, F. – (1996). *Counterpunch*. London: Hyphen Press.

Smith, F. – (1994). *Understanding Reading*. Hillsdale: Lawrence Erlbaum Associates.

Smith, M.M. – (1993). The pre-history of 'small caps': from all caps to smaller capitals to small caps, in: *Journal of the Printing Historical Society*. No. 22. London.

Southall, R. – (2005). *Printer's Type in the Twentieth Century*. London: The British Library.

Spencer, H. – (1968). *The Visible Word*. London: Lund Humphries Publishers Ltd.

Spencer, H. – (1969). *Pioneers of Modern Typography*. London: Lund Humphries Publishers Ltd.

Tankard, J. – (2005). *Kingfisher*. Lincoln: Jeremy Tankard Typography Ltd. http://typography. net/fontfamilies/view_sample/12

Tankard, J. – (2008). *TypeBookTwo*. Cambridge: Jeremy Tankard Typography Ltd.

Thibaudeau, F. – (1921). *La lettre d'imprimerie*. Paris: Au Bureau de l'Édition.

Tracy, W. – (1986). *Letters of Credit*. London: Gordon Fraser.

Tschichold, J. – (1925). Elementare Typographie, in *Typographische Mitteilungen*. Leipzig: Zeitschrift des Bildungsverbandes der Deutschen Buchdrucker.

Tschichold, J. – (1928). *Die neue Typographie*. Berlin: Verlag des Bildungsverbandes der Deutschen Buchdrucker.

Tschichold, J. – (1942). *Schriftkunde, Schreibübungen und Skizzieren für Setzer*. Basel: Benno Schwabe & Co.

Tschichold, J. – (1956). *Geschichte der Schrift in Bildern*. Basel: Holbein-Verlag.

Tschichold, J. – (1992). *Schriften 1925–1974*. Berlin: Brinkmann & Bose.

Turner Berry, W., A.F. Johnson, W.P. Jaspert. – (1962). *The Encyclopaedia of Typefaces*. London: Blandford Press.

Turner Berry, W., E. Edmund Poole. – (1966). *Annals of Printing*. London: Blandford Press.

Twomey, J. Spohn – (1989). On type: whence Jenson, a search for the origin of roman type, in: *Fine Print*. Vol. 15, No. 3, San Francisco.

Twyman, M. – (1993). The bold idea: the use of bold-looking types in the nineteenth century, in: *Journal of the Printing Historical Society*. No. 22. London.

Ullman, B.L. – (1960). *The Origin and Development of Humanistic Script*. Rome: Edizioni di Storia e Letteratura.

Unger, G.A. – (1979). The design of a typeface, in: *Visible Language,* Vol XIII, No. 2. Cleveland OH: Visible Language.

Unger, G.A. – (1981). Experimental No. 223, in: *Quærendo*. Vol. XI, No. 4. Amsterdam: Nico Israel.

Unger, G.A. – (2001). The types of François-Ambroise Didot and Pierre-Louis Vafflard. A further investigation into the origins of the Didones, in: *Quærendo,* Vol. 31, No. 3, Leiden: Koninklijke Brill NV.

Unger, G.A. – (2006). *Terwijl je leest*. Amsterdam: De Buitenkant. (2006). *Il gioco della lettura*. Viterbo: Nuovi Equilibri. (2007). *While You're Reading*. New York: Mark Batty Publisher. (2009). *Wie man's liest*. Zürich: Verlag Niggli. (2009). *¿Qué ocurre mientras lees?*. València: Campgràfic. (2015). *Pendant la lecture*. Paris: Éditions B42. Korean translation (2013), Seoul: Workroom Press. (2016). *Enquanto você lê*. Brasilia: Estereográfica.

Unger, G.A. – (1979). Romanesque capitals in inscriptions, in: *Typography Papers*, No. 9, London: Hyphen Press.

Updike, D.B. – (1962, originally 1922). *Printing Types*, vols I & II. Cambridge MA: Harvard University Press.

Van Blokland, E., J. van Rossum – (1991). Beowolf, in: *Emigre,* No. 18, Berkeley CA: Emigre Graphics.

Van Blokland, E., – (2015). Type & Media, in: *365 x typo*, Paris: étapes: editions

Vervliet, H.D.L. – (1968). *Sixteenth-Century Printing Types of the Low Countries*. Amsterdam: Menno Herzberger & Co.

Veyrin-Forrer, J. – (1987). Les premiers caractères de François-Ambroise Didot (1781–1785), in: *La lettre et le texte*. Paris: Collection de l'École Normale Supérieure de Jeunes Filles, No. 34.

Von Holdt, R. – (2013). *Morris Fuller Benton, Type Designer – Fact or Fiction?* apa-letterpress.com: Amalgamated Printers' Association.

Von Larisch, R. – (1913). *Unterricht in ornamentaler Schrift*. Vienna: K.K. Hof- und Staatsdruckerei.

Wallis, L.W. – (1990). *Modern Encyclopedia of Typefaces*. London: Lund Humphries Publishers Ltd.

Warde, B. – (1956). *The Crystal Goblet*. Cleveland: The World Publishing Company.

Wellek, R., A. Warren. – (1980). *Theory of Literature*. Middlesex: Penguin Books Ltd.

Wilk, C., et al. – (2006). *Modernism*. London: V&A Publications.

Willberg, H.P., F. Forssman. – (1997). *Lesetypographie*. Mainz: Verlag Hermann Schmidt.

Zachrisson, B. – (1965). *Studies in the Legibility of Printed Text*. Stockholm: Almqvist & Wiksell.

Glossary
of terms as used in this publication

Alternate – variant of a character in a font, often provided as a contextual or stylistic substitute.

Ascender – part of lowercase letters rising above the x-height, on **b**, **d**, **f**, **h**, **k** and **l**.

Asymmetry – an important ingredient of Modernist typography (along with sanserif typefaces) from the early twentieth century, and of its revival from the mid 1950s till the late 1970s (see Modernism). By contrast, traditional or classical typography is predominantly symmetrical.

Baroque – the style in the arts, architecture, design, and typography, which lasted from the latter decades of the sixteenth century into the first half the eighteenth century. Examples of Baroque type style are the roman types cut by Nicholas Kis (1650–1702) between 1680 and 1689 in Amsterdam.

Body copy – the main part of a text, apart from chapter headings, subheadings, footnotes and similar elements. In advertisements: the text apart from a headline.

Bold – a font or type style heavier than the basic or regular weight of a typeface, and distinctly different from it in weight. Often typefaces have a semi-bold, as well as weights heavier than the bold. There is no standard weight for bold – it depends on the type design and the distribution of the other weights within a type family.

Bracketed – describes a curved transition from stem to serif, instead of a sharp corner between them (see Clarendon and Egyptian).

Broad-nibbed pen – a pen with a flat or chisel-shaped ending for writing letterforms with a consistent difference between thick and thin parts and a gradual change from thin to thick, usually at an angle of about 30–40° (diagonal stress; see Old face).

Burin – a tool with a sharp ending (either pointed or spoon-shaped), used for cutting letterforms in steel to make punches.

Calligraphy – fine or artistic writing with pens or brushes, usually broad-nibbed. The guided action of the writing tool results directly in the final letter shapes, normally without further alteration. Modern calligraphers often experiment with any kind of tool that they can write with.

Capital – (majuscule, uppercase) letter derived from the Roman square capitals.

Carolingian minuscule – lowercase letterforms, developed in the second half of the eighth century in northern France, lauded for their clarity. The Carolingian minuscule was diffused throughout a large part of Europe by Charlemagne's patronage of education and scholarship. During the twelfth century it was slowly transformed into the Gothic script, and early in the fifteenth century the Carolingian letterforms were revived as the humanistic minuscule.

Cathode ray tube – a vacuum tube made of glass, containing one or more electron guns for displaying images on a phosphorescent screen. It was widely used in home television sets, computer screens, and also in early digital typesetting machines.

Clarendon – letterforms with bracketed slab serifs and a clear differentiation between thick and thin parts (see Ionic). These typefaces are often classified as Egyptians, although the latter generally have little or no difference between thick and thin, along with unbracketed serifs. Clarendons are the typical letterforms of the Industrial Revolution.

Classicism – a movement in the arts and architecture developed during the Renaissance that has endured ever since. It continued to play a prominent part in the seventeenth, eighteenth and nineteenth century, and was revived in the twentieth century as Modern Classicism (or New Traditionalism). It can be described as a regard for the arts and architecture (and also the literature and philosophy) of ancient Greece and Rome, characterized by harmony, restraint and clarity.

Coherence – concerns the relationships between fonts and the interplay of all variations of characters in a typeface. Coherence and consistency overlap in meaning, but coherence is the broader concept of the two. Consistency concerns more the details of signs within a font and their relationship to similar details in the other fonts of a typeface.

Colour – here colour means tonal value, which is determined by the relative weights of the parts of a typeface, by the amounts of space that come with each character, and by the degree of complexity in a type design. It is a blend of the black (or another colour) of the letters with the background colour.

Composite part – the combination of several parts of a letterform or other typographic sign, for example a foot serif with part of a stem attached, or even half a letterform, that can be moved together and applied to various characters (see Modular).

Computer-to-plate – a page composed of text and images is sent from a computer to an imaging device and output directly to a printing plate, without any intermediate phase such as photographic reproduction. The CTP technology has greatly improved the quality of printing.

Consistency – see coherence.

Contrast – difference in weight between the thick and thin parts of a typeface; little difference means a low contrast while a great difference means a strong contrast.

Control point – a point on the digital contour of a letterform or other typographic sign – a corner, curve, or tangent point – which allows the contour to be encoded and manipulated.

Convention – the knowledge shared by readers of a particular script, the generally accepted forms of letters and other characters. This know-how, embedded in the brain, ensures that reading is a custom, close to an automatism, and that readers have no difficulties processing the letters and lines of text while concentrating on its content. This is the social component of type design, dependent on reading as a widely practiced activity.

Counterpunch – a punch used for making the counter (interior blank space) of a letterform sculpted in metal, such as the space inside **a b** or **n**.

Craft – making things by hand, requiring particular skills and knowledge. Having
all phases of making something in one's own hands: planning, execution,
and production.

Currency symbol – a symbol representing a currency's name, such as **£** for pound sterling.

Cyrillic script – an alphabet used for various languages across eastern Europe and north
and central Asia, especially for Russian. Bulgarians use several alternative characters
and others have been added for Asian languages.

Descender – part of letters extending below the baseline: on lowercase **g, j, p, q,** and **y;**
and sometimes on capitals **J** and **Q**.

Design – for industry, design means mainly planning and drawing or visualizing a product,
while in type design digitization has brought production – the finishing of fonts and
preparing these for various applications – into the hands of designers (see Craft).

Desktop publishing – (DTP) creating documents on a computer screen, to be printed or
displayed on screen, and involving typographic and graphic design skills.

Diacritic – a mark placed over, under, next to, or through a letter to change the phonetic
value of that letter. Some diacritics, such as the ´ (acute) are called accents.

Digital outline – the contour of a letterform, based on and anchored to a digital grid
of horizontal and vertical lines – 1000 x 1000, for example. The outline is a virtual
representation of mathematical descriptions of a letter's shape.

Digital typesetting – the process of setting type with a keyboard and making it appear
on the screen of a computer or another digital device, to be then printed or displayed
on screen.

Display face – a typeface made more to look at than to be read, and to be used in
fairly large to very large sizes. There is no precise definition of a display typeface:
they are often outspoken, eccentric, show fancy traits ostentatiously, and can be
unconventional and even inconsistent, to some extent. This may affect their legibility
and can render them unfit for text in small sizes.

Egyptian – letterforms with slab serifs and little or no differentiation between thick and
thin parts. Usually their serifs are unbracketed and have optically the same thickness
as other horizontal parts of the letters. Serifs can be rectangular as well as trapezoid.
(See Clarendon.)

Ergonomics – the applied science of making things easy to use for humans. Here it
concerns an effective interaction between readers and typographic signs, to enable
easy and speedy reading, and to aid the comprehension of a text.

Expansion – (in the usage by Gerrit Noordzij) strictly vertical-horizontal difference
between the thick and thin parts of letterforms, characteristic of the modern face. It
is the outcome of applying pressure, while writing, on a pointed and flexible nib, with
widening strokes as a consequence.

Eye fixation – the moment the eyes are fixated on a bit of text, between saccades (eye
movements). During a fixation – a fifth or a quarter of a second for most readers – the
eyes pick up from four to about eighteen characters, including spaces between words.

Fat face – an extremely bold style of modern face developed at the beginning of the nineteenth century, with extreme contrast between thick and thin strokes.

Figure – see Numeral.

Fitting – allocating the amounts of space on both sides of each character in a font so that in any combination, in all words and lines of text, and in all languages (using the Latin script), the inter-character spaces are well-balanced with the internal spaces of all characters, and comfortably legible lines of text are formed, with an agreeable rhythm.

Font – a font is a complete set of characters in one single style or weight: for instance, all the characters in the light roman version of a particular typeface. In the days of metal type it was a complete set of characters for a particular variant cast at a specific size. In Britain it was spelled 'fount'.

Font format – variety of software encoding all the characters in a font. For example, PostScript, TrueType, OpenType.

Formalization – the process of reaching a consistent form or shape for letters and accompanying signs. When, from around 1450, letters were cast in metal in large numbers from one and the same matrix, variation drastically decreased, compared to handwriting. Since then, formalization has steadily increased.

French curve – a template made from metal, wood or plastic representing one of many different curves, used in manual drafting.

Genre – a kind or category of text, such as a novel, a poem, or an academic article.

Glyph – the particular version of a character. The basic shape of the A, for example, appears in many different guises as glyphs. Type designers make glyphs.

Gothic – generic term for 'broken scripts' – in other words, styles of Latin script in which curves are generally broken, as opposed to the commonly round curves of roman. Mostly characterized by strong contrast between thick and thin strokes, and often giving a dark overall colour to text (hence another English term for gothic, 'Blackletter'). Historical varieties of gothic are: Textura, Rotunda, Schwabacher, and Fraktur (Civilité was kind of gothic cursive.) Gothic type was used widely in Europe until the eighteenth century but, by the early twentieth century, Germany was the last bastion of gothic type (principally Fraktur). The term gothic was also used around the turn of the twentieth century in the USA to refer to sanserif types (for example, *News Gothic*).

Graphic designer – a professional who combines text (as typography), images, two-dimensional space, colour, and different materials such as paper and cardboard, to create a design according to a plan, and to be realized – multiplied – by printers, binders, and others within the graphic industry. Nowadays it increasingly concerns digital forms of visual information.

Greek script – the alphabet used to represent the Greek language.

Grid – a framework made up of horizontal and vertical lines, a basis for layouts and type designs.

Grotesque – an early designation of typefaces without serifs, also known as gothic (in the USA), which are referred to as sanserif in this book. Originally the term meant strangely ugly or bizarre. Later it became the label for a particular kind of sanserif from the end of the nineteenth century, such as *Akzidenz Grotesk*, with a modern-face structure. Later designs like *Helvetica* have been labeled as neo-grotesque.

Headline – text atop an article, usually in a large type size, especially in newspapers, magazines and advertisements. A short text at the top of a chapter in a book is not a headline but a title.

Humanist (or humanistic) – in typography this term is used to identify early roman typefaces, or designs based on these, with an old-face structure and still close to humanistic handwriting in deportment. The term is also used in connection with sanserifs with an old-face structure.

Humanistic minuscule – handwriting of Italian humanists, developed from the early fifteenth century and modelled on the Carolingian minuscule.

Hybrid – a type design whose elements are derived from different origins, such as an upright italic with the serif formation of a roman, or a type design containing elements of both Fraktur (a kind of gothic) and roman.

Immersive reading – also called sustained or deep reading; concerns the reading of substantial quantities of text, causing you to concentrate, and taking up most if not all of your attention, to the point of excluding other perceptions or activities.

Indent – a small amount of white space to indicate the beginning of a paragraph.

Informal – a roman (upright typeface) with some characteristics of italic, especially in the a, e and g. This member of a type family was developed in the late 1980s.

Initial – the first and enlarged letter of a text, often decorated. One of the means to indicate the beginning of a chapter.

Inscriptional – letterforms as found in inscriptions, such as Roman square capitals (see Lapidary).

Intercharacter space – the space between two characters and the sum of two sidebearings, on the right of the first letter and on the left of the second letter.

Interlinear space – the space between lines of text, often measured from baseline to baseline, consisting of the type size, sometimes with additional space. If a typeface has a large x-height, for example, interlinear space may be increased, just as it may be in order to aid the reading of text with a wide measure (long lines). Added interlinear space used to be called leading, originally consisting of strips of lead inserted between lines of metal type, although leading is now often synonymous with interlinear space in desktop publishing.

Ionic – a designation for letterforms similar to Clarendon. Later it became the name of a famous Linotype newspaper typeface (1925).

Italian/Italienne – a kind of display typeface with a reversed contrast – the strokes that are conventionally thin are made thick, and vice versa.

Italic – the sloping companion of the upright or roman version of a typeface, with its own characteristics. Italics are mostly somewhat condensed, compared with roman, and often a little lighter, with in- and out-going upstrokes at the top and bottom of the x-height, and roman-like serifs on the ends of vertical parts, especially ascenders, descenders, and in capitals.

Kerning – the adjustment of space between pairs of characters that would otherwise leave a gap in a word or a line of text (To) or would be too close for comfort (r:).

Laid paper – paper made with a mould (a kind of sieve) in which wires are laid side by side (see Wove paper).

Lapidary – having characteristics of letters cut in stone (see Inscriptional).

Laser printer – a printer, often small, that uses the light beam of a laser to project text and images on a rotating drum before electrostatically transferring these to paper with toner.

Latin script – a set of graphic signs, stemming mainly from three different sources. The capitals are the descendants of Roman square capitals, the model for the lowercase was the humanistic minuscule, and the numerals were borrowed from the Arabs during the high Middle Ages. It is supposedly used by about 70% of the world's population.

Layout – the way in which text, images and accompanying space are arranged on a page or screen.

Legibility – The English language includes both 'legibility' and 'readability'. Simply put, readability is the domain of authors and editors, legibility that of type designers, typographers, graphic and website designers.

Letterform – the shape of a letter (not only of the Latin script), either written or designed as part of a typeface.

Letterpress – printing from a raised, relief surface, traditionally from movable type, but also encompassing more recent techniques such as stereotyping and photo-etched printing blocks.

Light – here a font or type style lighter than the basic weight of a typeface (the regular), and distinctly different from it in weight. There is no standard weight for light, and variations may extend further as thin, ultra light, or ultra thin.

Lowercase – the members of a typeface modeled after the humanistic minuscule, a kind of writing developed early in the fifteenth century and which in turn was based on the Carolingian minuscule. Lowercase refers to the lower of two cases (drawers) of metal type used by a compositor. The upper case contained the capital letters.

Macrotypography – the larger scale aspects of typography, coinciding with layout. Arranging textual elements such as parts of a main text and footnotes or captions in relation to other elements, mostly images and space.

Majuscule – the term for a capital in paleography (the study of ancient written characters).

Matrix – the hollow representation of a letterform in bronze, struck from a steel punch on which the original version of a letter has been cut in relief. Metal type can be cast from a matrix in a large quantity.

Microtypography – the small-scale aspects of typography, the detailing of text, such as managing wordspaces and interlinear space, the use of punctuation marks, lining or old style numerals, etcetera.

Minuscule – the term for small letters (lowercase) in paleography.

Modern face – a kind of typeface with a marked difference between thick and thin parts, strictly vertical-horizontal. This contrast is derived from the effects of using a pointed and flexible pen while applying pressure, spreading the nib, with widening strokes as a consequence (see Expansion). Modern faces were first made around 1784 in France.

Modernism – in graphic design, beginning in the mid 1920s, it relies heavily on the use of sanserif typefaces, dynamic and asymmetrical layouts, the use of photography and collage for images, and the integration of imagery and typography. This movement was fuelled by the idea that the world could be changed and freed of history and tradition. In the mid-1950s these ideas were in part revived and revised and led to what was called 'Swiss typography', a severely programmatic approach of graphic design and typography with a prominent role for grids, and *Helvetica* and *Univers*.

Modular – type design with standardized, interrelated, and repeatable components.

Monolinear – a typeface with vertical and horizontal parts of the same visual weight.

Monospaced – a typeface with all characters fitted on the same width of space (including their sidebearings). This means severe compression of wide characters such as m, M, w and W, and the widening of narrow characters like i, l, r or 1. In a text these characters will line up both vertically and horizontally.

Neoclassicism – the revival of Classicism from the mid-eighteenth century (see Classicism).

Newspaper typeface – (newsface) a heavy-duty typeface for newspapers, designed to withstand stereotyping and rotary printing with thin ink on rough and tinted paper. (Stereotyping is the process of making a semicylindrical, relief printing plate from the flat forme of a made-up newspaper page, with a cardboard matrix as an intermediate step.) Later such typefaces also had to endure repeated photographic reproduction.

New Typography – term used from around 1925 during the development of Modernist graphic design (see Modernism). It was codified in Jan Tschichold's eponymous and iconic book *Die neue Typographie* (1928), propagating a wider use of sanserif typefaces, asymmetrical and dynamic typography, the integration of text and images, and more. This was originally a European development, involving elements of several movements in the arts, such as Futurism, Constructivism, and Dadaism. In the late 1930s it spread to the United States as many representatives of this movement fled Europe.

Non-ranging numerals – numerals of different heights, extending above and below the x-height, to be combined with lowercase letters (1234567890). Also called old-style or text numerals.

Numeral – a symbol representing a digit (0–9). In the system of 'Roman numerals' capital letters represent numbers.

Oblique – slanted roman letters, accompanying some sanserif romans (Grotesques) instead of italic. Electronically or digitally slanted romans need much correction to become good-looking oblique letterforms.

Old face – a kind of roman typeface with a difference between thick and thin parts at an angle of approximately 30–45°. This contrast is derived from the effects of using a broad-nibbed pen at a more or less fixed angle in relation to the writing line or baseline. Old face covers a long period from shortly after the invention of printing up to the typefaces of William Caslon I and Pierre-Simon Fournier le jeune from the first half of the eighteenth century. (See Renaissance roman.)

Old Style – often used as synonymous with old face, but actually the name of a nineteenth-century typeface. It was cut by Alexander Phemister and published in 1860 by Miller & Richard in Edinburgh. It is also a term used for non-ranging numerals.

OpenType – (1996) a combination of two font formats, Postscript and TrueType, that can contain many more characters than both previous font formats, and offers typographic subtleties such as small caps, non-ranging numerals, and alternate characters.

OpenType Variable Fonts – (2016) a substantial extension of OpenType which makes it possible to contain almost unlimited variations of a type family within a single, compactly packaged font file. A variable font is a single font file that behaves like multiple fonts.

Optical adjustment – the correction of an optical illusion such as an o seeming to be too small compared to an x, if the curves at the top and bottom of the o do not protrude a little beyond the top and bottom of the x.

Overshoot – the extent to which parts of some letters, mainly curves, protrude above and below the x-height or the capital height.

Paleography – the study of ancient written characters.

Pantograph – an instrument for the reduction (or enlarging) of drawings which, combined with an engraving machine, made possible the manufacture of punches and matrices in a variety of type sizes from a large template.

Paperback – a book with a flexible paper or cardboard binding, glued at the back.

Paragraph – a section of a written or typeset text beginning on a new, usually indented line (now often after a blank line), and usually consisting of several sentences dealing with a single thought or topic.

Pattern – a regular repetition of verbal, graphic elements: recurring combinations of letters in words; repeated sequences of words; customary combinations of nouns and adjectives; the accepted positions of adverbs, prepositions, etc. Language, with grammar and syntax, is the driving force behind the pattern that a typeface can form. (See Rhythm.)

Phonetic symbol – a sign representing a spoken sound. The letters of the Latin script represent sounds, as do the special signs of the International Phonetic Alphabet, a system of phonetic notation based on the Latin alphabet.

Phototypesetting – setting text by projecting typographic characters from negatives through lenses onto photographic film or paper. This technology, used mainly from the early 1960s till the late 1980s, enormously increased the speed of output in comparison to typesetting machines processing hot metal. Early cathode-ray-tube typesetters were also a kind of phototypesetting machine (see Cathode ray tube). Indeed, most digital output still normally includes an element of photography, given that light-sensitive paper, film, or plate is exposed by a laser.

Postscript – together with TrueType, a font format used before the introduction of OpenType.

Pragmatism – here a practical, problem-solving approach to type design.

Printing plate – the text-and-image-bearing element in the process of offset printing. The inked text and images are transferred from the plate to a rubber blanket, and then onto paper. Offset printing is a planographic process – in other words, the printable parts are in the same plane as the non-printing parts on the plate (see Letterpress).

Punch – a piece of steel on top of which a letterform (or other typographic sign) is cut in relief by chiseling with burins, filing, and applying counterpunches. Punches were cut by hand at actual size (and later mechanically by pantographic tracing of a larger pattern). After hardening the steel, the punch was stamped into a piece of brass. From the resulting matrix, fixed in a mould, type was cast.

Punchcutting – the making of a punch by cutting and filing away part of a steel rod.

Punctuation mark – a mark or sign, such as the comma (,) or the colon (:), for insertion in a text to aid the understanding of that text.

Ranging numerals – numerals of equal height, also called lining numerals. These can have the same height as the capitals but can also be slightly shorter. No parts of them descend below the baseline. (See also Tabular numerals.)

Readability – the domain of authors and editors; how a text is written and edited (see Legibility).

Renaissance roman – a designation for early roman typefaces, made in Venice from around 1465 till around the mid-sixteenth century in Paris, cut by, among others, Nicolas Jenson (if we assume he cut his own types), Francesco Griffo, and Claude Garamond.

Resolution – the number of pixels (picture elements) per inch (or another measuring unit) in digital typesetting machines, laserprinters, and screen displays, which determines the level of detail that these technologies can present to the human eye.

Retina display – a display developed by Apple, having a higher pixel density than traditional displays, so that the pixels are not visible to the naked eye.

Rhythm – in type design, a visual impression created by the sequential recurrence of similar and contrasting letter shapes, combined with the spaces within and between them. Alfred North Whitehead once defined rhythm as a 'fusion of sameness and novelty'; in other words, it is not equivalent to mere repetition, although a dominant aspect of rhythm in type design is the regular repetition of the main vertical elements of letterforms. (See also Pattern and Texture.)

Roman – generic name for the now dominant styles of the Latin script, derived originally from humanist handwriting and Roman inscriptional capitals, and subsequently developed in many varieties by type designers. Roman typefaces are normally seriffed (see sanserif). The term may also signify upright as opposed to italic, and is also used as synonymous with regular. if 'Roman' is written with an initial capital, it refers to ancient Rome: for example, 'Roman capitals' are those made in ancient Rome, whereas 'roman capitals' are simply the capitals of a roman typeface.

Roman Republican capitals – monolinear and sometimes constructed letterforms with minimal serifs (or without them entirely) from before 100 ad; these are the predecessors of the seriffed Roman (Imperial) square capitals.

Sanserif – without serifs (see Serif; Grotesque).

Scotch face – or Scotch roman, a kind of typeface with a high contrast and bracketed serifs from the early nineteenth century, originally made in Glasgow and Edinburgh. This kind of typeface later became popular in the USA, where the term 'Scotch' became attached to it.

Scribe – a copyist of manuscripts.

Script – a type design derived from studied writing, showing the influence of pencil, pen, different kinds of brush – or any instrument that can be turned into a writing tool; and often with fluid movements as a consequence of rapid writing. Also: a particular writing system, such as cuneiform.

Semantic differential – a rating scale for measuring possible meanings, intended or not, that can be associated with type designs (and other objects). It is based on opposing characteristics such as rich and poor, male and female, or active and passive.

Semantics – the science or study of meaning in language, also of the signs representing language.

Serif – a protruding part appearing at the ends of the main vertical, horizontal, and diagonal sections of letters. They can be more or less triangular or trapezoid in shape (old face); or straight and thin (modern face), or straight and heavy in Egyptians. Originally added to written letterforms as a separate stroke or as the result of a continued movement of a pen or brush.

Serif formation – the specific distribution of serifs throughout a typeface in fixed places, such as: triangular serifs at the tops of ascenders (**l, b, h**) and at the top of the x-height (**n, p**); horizontal serifs on capitals and in lowercase on diagonals (**v**), along the baseline, and at the ends of descenders. Serifs may have many shapes but can nearly always be found in the specified locations.

Sidebearing – a space on one side of a typographic character, defined by the designer or producer of a font and part of the total horizontal space occupied by that character. Each character has two sidebearings (on the left and on the right).

Signage – directional signs, such as for traffic.

Slant – a direction deviating from the perpendicular, leaning towards the right in type design for the Latin script; also called slope (see Oblique).

Small capitals – letters with the forms of capitals, but only slightly taller than the lowercase letters and to be combined with these; used for acronyms, emphasis, as an alternative for italic, for running heads or subtitles in books, and other typographic duties. Proper small capitals are not simply full-height capitals reduced in size but are redesigned to harmonize with the weight and proportions of the lowercase.

Spacing – this can be the addition of equal amounts of extra space between all the letters of a word, a title or a similar text (see Tracking). It can be done optically also, by adding and taking away space between certain letter combinations to achieve well balanced inter-character spaces.

Square capitals – Roman Imperial capital letters, or *capitalis quadrata*, used by the Romans from the first century ad. Essentially, we still use these letterforms, which were revived by scribes early in the fifteenth century and combined with the humanistic minuscule; and then this pairing was fixed by the first roman types.

Stencil – a sheet of cardboard or plastic, in which letterforms have been cut out with bridging links, so that the counters do not fall out. Ink or paint can be applied through the openings to a surface beneath.

Stereotyping – from a newspaper page, composed in metal type and locked flat in a forme, an impression was made in a sheet of cardboard (making a flong or matrix), from which was cast a semicylindrical printing surface for rotary printing. As a flong was force-dried in an oven, it shrunk, and so the type would become smaller.

Stroke – a trace of a pen made with a single uninterrupted movement of the hand. Used to describe the principal parts of letterforms in type design.

Structure – the interrelation and customary arrangement of all parts of a type design. Also the supporting structure of dimensions on which a type design is based.

Subheading – a heading of a subsection in a text; or a secondary heading, adding information to a headline (also known as a subtitle).

Tabular numerals – monospaced numerals to be ranged vertically for use in tables of figures. These can be both ranging numerals (of equal height) or non-ranging numerals (also called old-style or lowercase numerals).

Template – a pattern, such as a thin metal plate, with the slightly raised shape of a letter or other sign, used as a guide for a pantograph in the mechanical cutting of punches.

Terminal – a mark at an extremity of a letterform or another sign, such as at the top left of an a. Terminals can be ball shaped, triangular, or have various other shapes. Terminal is generally used to refer to shapes that are not serifs, although serifs are also a kind of terminal.

Text face – normally a fairly quiet and conventional typeface used to set text for immersive or deep reading, for books and the main texts of newspapers and magazines, and also for longer texts on screens.

Texture – the visual effect of the interplay of all parts of a typeface in small sizes, often referred to by typographers as the 'colour' of a typeset text. The difference between texture and pattern is limited; it is a matter of scale, of the size of a text and of the distance from reader to text. (See also Rhythm.)

Tracking – the uniform enlargement or reduction of the spaces between all the characters in a text, or segment of a text (see Spacing).

Transitional – typefaces with both old-face and modern-face characteristics (such as top serifs at an angle combined with a modern-face contrast), made during the eighteenth century. The best-known example is *Baskerville*.

Translation – (in the usage by Gerrit Noordzij) the articulation of difference between thick and thin parts of old-face letterforms; the outcome of moving a broad-nibbed pen at a more or less fixed angle (30–45°) in relation to the writing line or baseline.

TrueType – together with Postscript, a font format used before the introduction of OpenType.

Type – this was the term used for metal letters to be composed for letterpress printing. It referred to them collectively or generally, as in typecasting or a typewriter. It is now used also for digitally made letters.

Typecasting – type was cast in a mould, containing a matrix.

Type design – the design of typographic letterforms and other signs; also referred to as typeface design. The fact that 'type' is the object of design implies that letters *per se* are not the purpose, but rather unified groups of letters and other typographic characters (fonts and groups of fonts).

Typeface – a set of fonts of the same or related design.

Typeface design programme – an educational course, usually an MA.

Type family – a group of related fonts, roman and italic, from light to black, all with the same characteristics or interpretations thereof. The designation family often refers to a larger group of fonts than those in a typeface. There is the extended type family, wherein several scripts can work together.

Type metal – the alloy used in typefounding and hot-metal typesetting, consisting mainly of lead, with antimony added for hardness, and tin for fluidity.

Type specimen – printed leaflet, brochure, or book with examples of typefaces in the sizes cast by a particular typefoundry. Specimens on the web are much more flexible and often include the possibility to try out fonts.

Typographer – a practitioner of typography (not of type design). A designer who devises a plan for this kind of work. Before the mid-1980s such a plan was often effectuated by others working in the graphic industry. The personal computer has brought execution of the plan into the hands of the designer.

Typography – the arrangement and detailing of text (combined with images and space) according to a premeditated plan, originally for printing on paper (as in books and newspapers), and now also for screen display.

Ultra black – an extremely heavy weight of a typeface.

Uncials – a Latin script with letterforms referred to as majuscules, although its rounded shapes and some short ascending and descending parts foreshadow minuscule letterforms. It originated in the second century AD and by the fourth century uncials were widely used. (Latin uncials were preceded by Greek uncials.)

Unicode – an international standard for the encoding, representation, and handling of characters of most – ultimately of all – of the world's writing systems, including historical scripts and all symbols.

Upstrokes – upward strokes making a smooth transition from stem to curve (on n, h, etc) in many roman typefaces, and conventionally thinner than the stems. They are often more pronounced in italic fonts, reflecting their derivation from cursive writing, and sometimes begin almost at the base of the stem (the current author's *Flora* [1984] is a cursive sanserif with extremely prominent upstrokes). Italics of seriffed typefaces generally feature short in- and outgoing upstrokes at the top and bottom of thick (down) strokes bounded by the x-height (e.g. on i and n).

Web – the World Wide Web is an information space where documents and other resources are identified by Uniform Resource Locators (url), connected by hypertext links, and accessible via the Internet.

Web Open Font Format – (woff) the font format for use in web pages, supported by all browsers. The fonts are compressed, so they occupy less bandwidth and will load faster than uncompressed fonts.

Website – a set of related web pages under one domain name.

Word processing – the production, manipulation, and storage of text by capturing data with a keyboard and arranging it in a program running on a computer, resulting in a printout or text displayed on a screen. A kind of computerized typewriting with the added advantage of storage in flexible, digital formats.

Wove paper – Wove paper is made with a mould (a kind of sieve) in which the wires are woven together like the threads of cloth, as distinct from laid paper, where the wires are laid side by side (see Laid paper). The papermaker James Whatman has been credited with the introduction of wove paper around 1757.

x-height – one of the main dimensions in a type design, together with the height of the capitals. It is the basic height of the lowercase letters, minus ascenders, descenders, and overshoots. The x-height can vary in terms of its proportion of the total height of a typeface, and it does not have a fixed position within that height.

Index

Sources

of texts used in type illustrations

15   http://www.bbc.com/news/world-europe-23072361
46   Insights and Oversights of the Great Thinkers: An Evaluation of Western …
     By Charles Hartshorne, page 78
62   http://www.guppyfishtank.com/are-guppies-egg-laying-fish/
66   https://saltmagazine.asia/pickmeupmondays/emperors-superfood-birds-nest/
74   https://www.quora.com/What-is-a-distant-relative
75   https://www.forbes.com/sites/ethansiegel/2015/07/01/
     the-only-three-heavy-elements-in-the-universe-that-arent-made-in-stars/
76   https://en.wikipedia.org/wiki/Superimposition
78   https://www.jstor.org/stable/3129415?seq=1#page_scan_tab_contents
79   https://nl.wikipedia.org/wiki/Christoffel_van_Dijck
79   https://pureheavenly.com
80, 81   https://pdfs.semanticscholar.org/17b0/9788c100e6fad5ccefd61e0067da734cab5a.pdf
82   https://en.wikipedia.org/wiki/Egyptian_geometry
82   https://en.wikipedia.org/wiki/Newspaper
83   https://en.wikipedia.org/wiki/Concrete
83   https://en.wikipedia.org/wiki/Rock_(geology)
86   Helen Saberi, Alan Davidson – Trifle, Prospect Books 2001
88   https://www.ldoceonline.com/dictionary/otherworldly
88   http://www.casinoreviewsquad.com/betting-systems/the-paroli-betting-system
95   http://www.historyofinformation.com/expanded.php?id=2422
104   https://en.wikipedia.org/wiki/Diotima_of_Mantinea
110   https://study.com/academy/lesson/hypothesis-theory-law-in-science.html
113   http://myths.e2bn.org/mythsandlegends/textonly13478-the-legend-of-robin-hood.html
114   https://teklastructures.support.tekla.com/2017i/en/mod_creating_horizontal_parts
117   https://www.vocabulary.com/dictionary/intact
120   https://en.wikipedia.org/wiki/Squirrel
122   https://www.merriam-webster.com/dictionary/partial
129   David Crystal, How Language Works, 2005, Avery.
134   Pattern Illustrating Patterns: A Pattern Language for Pattern Illustrating –
     By Takashi Iba, Iba Laboratory
137   https://practicaltypography.com/bold-or-italic.html
139   https://en.wikipedia.org/wiki/Independence_(probability_theory)
139   https://unity3d.com/learn/tutorials/topics/scripting/
     how-communicate-between-scripts-and-gameobjects
140   Effect of sloped text upon the readability of print, Tinker Miles A.,
     Optometry and Vision Science: April 1956 - Volume 33 - Issue 4 - ppg 189–195
140   http://www.leeds.ac.uk/educol/documents/000000723.htm
144   https://en.wikipedia.org/wiki/Miller
144   https://wordsinasentence.com/rudimentary-in-a-sentence/
151   https://www.theguardian.com/film/2018/jan/21/the-post-observer-film-review
160   https://www.brainyquote.com/quotes/linus_torvalds_587390
175   https://www.cnbc.com/2017/08/08/the-best-fonts-to-use-on-a-resume-according-
     to-designers.html
180   http://www.allaboutvision.com/over40/presbyopia-options.htm
184   https://www.keleem.com/collections/collections/products/triangle-contrast-1
192   http://meera.snre.umich.edu/evaluation-what-it-and-why-do-it
198   https://www.isixsigma.com/implementation/change-management-implementation/
     keeping-change-three-dimensional-view/
199   http://www.dictionary.com/browse/hybrid
209   https://en.wikipedia.org/wiki/Homeland

Credits

Texts	Gerard Unger
Editing	Christopher Burke
Design	Hansje van Halem
Typefaces	Alverata, Sanserata, Demos
Lithography and Printing	Wilco Art Books
Binding	Boekbinderij Van Waarden
Endpapers	printed by Offsetdrukkerij Jan de Jong
Paper	Wibalin (cover), Munken Premium Cream (interior), Magno Volume (endpapers)
Production	Brecht Bleeker
Publisher	nai010 publishers

This publication was made possible by financial support from
the creative industries fund NL, J.E. Jurrriaanse Fonds/Volkskracht
De Gijselaar-Hintzenfonds, Frederik Mullerfonds/Dr. P.A. Tiele-Stichting,
M.A.O.C. Gravin van Bylandt Stichting

creative industries fund NL   *J.E. Jurriaanse Stichting* Ⓥ   De Gijselaar-Hintzenfonds

Illustration credits

207 top – © Constantin Brancusi/Pictoright. Purchased with support from
the Ministry of Education, Culture and Science, the Mondriaan Fund and
the Rembrandt Association, partly thanks to the Prins Bernhard Cultuurfonds.
207 bottom – © Ellsworth Kelly

Although every effort was made to find the
copyright holders for the illustrations used,
it has not been possible to trace them all.
Interested parties are requested to contact
nai010 publishers, Mauritsweg 23, 3012 JR
Rotterdam, the Netherlands.

nai010 publishers is an internationally ori-
entated publisher specialized in developing,
producing and distributing books in the fields
of architecture, urbanism, art and design.
www.nai010.com

nai010 books are available internationally at
selected bookstores and from the following
distribution partners:
– North, Central and South America - Artbook |
  D.A.P., New York, USA, *dap@dapinc.com*
– Rest of the world - Idea Books, Amsterdam,
  the Netherlands, *idea@ideabooks.nl*

For general questions, please contact nai010
publishers directly at *sales@nai010.com* or
visit our website *www.nai010.com* for further
information.

Printed and bound in the Netherlands

ISBN 978-94-6208-440-7

Bisac DES007050

Theory of Type Design is also available
as an e-book
Theory of Type Design e-book (pdf)
ISBN 978-94-6208-451-3